#1 AMAZON INTERNATIONAL BESTSELLER

THE DRIVE TO ADVANCE

Master the Art of Leading Your Life

ALLAN MANDINDI

Foreword by Dr. Josephine Ojiambo

Scriptures quotations marked, unless otherwise indicated, are taken from the Holy Bible, the New International Version, and the King James Version KJV of the Holy Bible.

Amb. Allan Mandindi's Book titles may be purchased in bulk for Educational, Ministerial, Business, fundraising, or Sales Promotional use.

For information, please email- allanmandindi@gmail.com
Phone: +447969216335

Printed in the United Kingdom
ISBN:978-978-58812-1-9

Designed & published by

YPN
PUBLISHING & MEDIA

Whatsapp +2348023768604,
Email: admin@ypnpublishers-media.com
https://ypnpublishers-media.com
@ypnpublishers

DEDICATION

To every young leader, teenager, solopreneur, and established group that deserves special help to succeed, flourish, and improve the lives of themselves, their peers, and future generations.

ACKNOWLEDGEMENT

The most rewarding experience of my entire life was writing this book and sharing not only the story of my own life but also the stories of other remarkable people. This book shares not only my story but also the stories of other remarkable people.

Throughout the entirety of this process, there has been a remarkable level of dedication, effort, cooperation, and comprehension displayed. I want to begin by expressing my gratitude and thanksgiving to God for everything that he has done to supply me with the ideas and the fortitude I need to see this project through. I am truly thankful for everything that he has done. The fact that Sonja and the kids have been there for me and have shown their support means the absolute world to me.

I'd like to give YPN Publishers & Media my sincere appreciation for the skillful way in which they took my words and turned them into a book and for the substantial investment of time and effort they made in this endeavor.

I would like to give a special shout out to my amazing wife Sonja and my beautiful kids Angelica and Sean. My beloved parents, Harrison and Qitekile, the wider Mandindi family who have been such a source of encouragement and support throughout my entire life. I thank them for everything they have done for me. I owe a debt of gratitude to the teachers at my early schools - Chilambula Primary , Kamzimbi Primary, Phwezi secondary schools not forgetting lecturers at Manchester Metropolitan University. These institutions prepared me for greatness. Let me also acknowledge the amazing communities I have come across both in Malawi and the United Kingdom. Finally, great appreciation to following people who have been great source of inspiration to me. The President of Malawi, Dr. Lazarus Chakwera; HRH Dr Clyde Rivers; Hon Dr Ken Zikhale Ng'oma;

Prof Psalm Ebube; Mark Adjei-kumi; Hon Lucy Powell MP; Lord Mayor Donna Ludford; Dr Godson Azu; H.E Amb Dr Josephine Ojiambo; Apostle Dr Stanley S Ndovie; Prophet Blessings Chapo; Amb Dr Neena Richie; Bishop Josephine Katenga Kaunda; Sherita Mandongwe; David Lynch; Dr. Janet Mather; Regina Khanum and colleagues at Malawi Heritage UK, Manchester City Council.

CONTENTS

FOREWORD

Throughout the last seven years, I've had the pleasure of working closely with Allan Mandindi. We initiated and fostered a thriving think tank, The London Political Summit, with a team of enthusiastic governance, human rights, and development professionals. This endeavour has been coloured by lessons in knowing each member of the team, harnessing both innovation and discipline, and believing and waiting for positive results. As a consequence, I've learned that Allan is a master at shaping human behaviour and assisting individuals and teams in delivering extraordinary results in tough environments and under time constraints.

INTRODUCTION

Have you ever had the thought that anything is holding you back from leading the life that you want to live? It's almost as if an invisible string is holding you back from taking the potentially dangerous steps that are necessary to attain the things you want in life.

You may have feelings of inadequacy at times when you believe that you have failed to complete certain tasks because of internal forces that are making it difficult for you to complete these tasks. The truth is that something is preventing you from progressing, but you are unable to see what it is. It is not anything that you can see. One further thing to keep in mind is that the aforementioned thing is not obscured from the view of the rest of the world. Because if it were invisible, the world around you would not respond to you in the same way that it does now. This fundamental truth, that the mind is a mirror, is unknown to a great number of individuals. What you constantly think about will reflect in the world, and people will treat you based on the quality of thoughts you process in your mind. This is true whether you realize it or not.

The majority of young people and aspiring leaders lose this opportunity because they are unaware that the change in thinking is the first step toward achieving the change they desire. Your mindset is the lens through which you see yourself and the world. It colours both of these experiences. As a consequence of this, it is the launching point for changes over a longer period. If you have feeble thinking, tremendous accomplishments in this world will be incredibly difficult to achieve for you.

The mind itself is a battlefield. This is the first step on the path to greatness. If you are successful as a soldier on the battlefield, you will emerge victorious, and the sands of time will eventually carve your footprints into the history books. As a result, make it a goal to triumph over this internal conflict that is subtle but significant. If you can conquer yourself, you will be able to conquer the world. What you pay attention to is what you become.

This book covers a wide range of methods for helping people improve their routines, behaviours, actions, and emotions. Consider the following examples to help you better understand the concept of personal development:

- Keeping yourself calm in stressful situations.
- How to break the habit of deferring things.
- How to get rid of laziness.
- Being more kind and respectful.
- Developing into a person with a greater sense of responsibility.
- Acquiring new knowledge and skills, as well as personal development.
- Changing your perspective and becoming more optimistic would both be good places to start.

To see changes in oneself, one must be motivated, have the desire to do better, and be willing to put in a lot of effort. You must also be willing to push yourself beyond your comfort zone and engage in unpleasant but necessary activities for your well-being. Furthermore, it is critical to keep an open mind and a strong desire to learn and grow.

The primary sources of influence on a person's ongoing process of personal development, which begins at a young age but continues throughout life, are their parents, teachers, and environment.

To get the most out of it, you must educate yourself on the procedure, understand what it entails, and work to develop and improve yourself in the appropriate ways.

At this point, I'd like to ask you these questions: how do you see yourself? Through the eyes of the rest of the world? What kinds of images do you have in your head all the time? Where exactly do you fall short?

There is no such thing as a perfect person! Every one of us has both positive and negative aspects to our personalities. Allow yourself to be immobilized by the flaws you have identified in yourself. You appreciate and enjoy your positive experiences while actively working to improve your negative ones. Your ability to improve while overcoming this mental challenge is what distinguishes you as a great person.

This subject is thoroughly covered throughout the book. The essence is to agitate you to help you see yourself differently because your mind must be prepared to see yourself as the great leader that God has chosen you to be. Don't believe your adversary's lies. Keep your head held high and believe you can achieve any goal you set for yourself if you put your mind to it. Develop an "I can do it" attitude in yourself.

This book will teach you how to update the software in your head so that you have more control over your life and the mental tools you need to overcome obstacles. I hope that by the end of this book, you will have a new perspective on yourself and your surroundings. In addition, we will show how having a positive mental attitude can take your life to a whole new level.

To achieve personal mastery and realize your dreams, you must cultivate what is known as a "mindset of greatness." Readers will gain an understanding of the greatness mindset held by the world's most successful and influential leaders. This book will teach you how to boost your self-esteem, develop mental toughness, and appreciate the unique characteristics that make up your personality.

You'll understand how to master your divine identity and sacred purpose and how to approach every day with joy and enthusiasm, how to use a positive mindset to accomplish more, how to harness the power of positive self-talk, how to act as a strong, inspiring leader for your loved ones and your team, how to become the unique individual God created you to be, how to win in life by a conscious choice, how the mind machine tends to work, how to reconnect with your full potential as a man, how to find your life's mission, who dares wins, danger and modern life. If you adopt the greatness attitude outlined in this book, you will be able to seize control of your life and triumph over any obstacles that stand in your way.

This book will teach you how to build your self-confidence, develop mental toughness, attack every day with joy and enthusiasm, use a positive mental attitude to achieve more, harness the power of positive self-talk, be a positive leader for your family and team, become the person you were born to be, why winning in life is a conscious choice, how the mind machine works, how you can reconnect with your full potential as a man, finding your life's mission, and who dares to succeed. You will be able to take charge of your life and triumph over any challenges you face with the help of the inspiration you find in this book.

What exactly is going on, hombre? Have you attempted something more than once but been unsuccessful? How often do you feel like no one loves you and that you are doomed to fail? Have you ever experienced feelings of depression or being out of shape? Do you find it difficult to keep your thoughts focused on the appropriate things? This book will show you how to access the resources that are already within you and how to use your imagination to create the life that you have always envisioned for yourself.

By reading this book, you will develop the knowledge and abilities necessary to better manage your feelings, thoughts, and behaviours to achieve your goals. You'll also get a better understanding of how maintaining a routine may lead to tremendous development in many facets of your life and ultimately influence the course of your path in life. After reading this book, you will be able to shift from having a pessimistic to an optimistic view, and despite the challenges you experience, you will be able to continue forward on the path of achieving your goals.

Perhaps you've been made to feel like an outcast and branded a failure in your life. The fact that it is not your name is very encouraging news. This book will show you how to access the power that you already possess and how to put it to use to accomplish what you set out to do in life. You have the ability to create and become anything you choose. This is not the time to give up on yourself, to entertain thoughts of suicide or to feel inferior to yourself or anyone else, or to view yourself as being on a lower level than anyone else. Find joy amid your sorrow; have hope even as you weep, knowing that you are in possession of something truly magnificent. Now is the time to recognize the greatness and power that are already present within you; to put to good use the talents and abilities that have lain dormant for far too long; to shed the stigma of failure from your shoulders; to find joy amid your sorrow; to find joy in the fact that you have failed. You are in possession of an invaluable treasure that no one should ever undervalue or ignore under any circumstance. You will be able to locate the buried treasure if you use the information that is included in this book. With the assistance of this enlightening book, you can acquire the skills necessary to face the obstacles you face daily with poise and confidence. As you read, you will get insight into the aspects of life that you have been neglecting.

"

Every successful person you ever come across has a story that can sweep you off your feet

– Allan Mandindi

"

CHAPTER 1

ESSENTIAL PERSPECTIVES OF LIFE

In order to get the most out of it, you need to educate yourself on the procedure, comprehend what it entails, and work to develop and better yourself in these appropriate ways.

Create no limits for the growth in your life. Sometimes adversity and challenges are all it takes to reawaken a dormant drive for personal development and pave the way toward making adjustments in one's life. When people read an inspirational book, see an inspiring movie, or read about successful people, it can occasionally encourage them to take steps toward their personal development.

People's lives are regularly altered as a result of this, as are their horizons of knowledge and self-awareness, as well as their capacity to acquire new abilities and hone those they already possess. Acquire knowledge about personal development. There is a plethora of material available in the form of books, articles, workshops, and coaches that are devoted to the subject of personal development.

The benefits of personal growth can be seen in many different facets of one's life. It could come in handy at the office. It has the potential to change your perspective on work, which in turn can lead to new prospects for promotion. Growing emotionally and mentally, as well as becoming a more compassionate, kind, and optimistic person, can all be helped along by engaging in personal development activities. In addition to this, it can assist you in recognizing your shortcomings and undesirable behaviors, enabling you to make the necessary adjustments and improvements.

Techniques for personal growth include meditation, creative imagery, repeating positive affirmations, cultivating a more optimistic outlook, and so on. Reading, therapy, and coaching are also important components of personal development. A very straightforward and efficient strategy for personal development is to examine one's actions and one's life with an objective and nonjudgmental mindset. This will highlight the changes that are necessary for you to make in both yourself and your life.

The act of watching the actions and behaviors of other people can also be beneficial. This enables you to distinguish between positive and negative character traits, become aware of whether you possess them or lack them, and so learn what it is about yourself that you need to work on improving. Because we are all unique, what works well for one person may not be effective at all for another. This indicates that you need to research a variety of strategies and approaches to personal growth in order to figure out which ones are most suitable for you.

- "We start maturing when we come to terms with our own frailties."
- Affirmations: If you want your life to be better, learn how to utilize affirmations to help you.
- Maintain a laser-like focus and attention on your own personal growth.
- Your personal growth might assist you in accomplishing your objectives.

You know those people who are always accomplishing incredible things, like going on several trips and obtaining new jobs that pay significantly more? Have you ever given any thought to the process that these "achievers" use? Is it possible that these agents of change are driven by the desire for personal development and accomplishment?

An emphasis on acquiring new knowledge, being open to new experiences, and according to certain viewpoints, actively pursuing one's own goals is what leads to personal development. A significant number of successful people continue to work hard at bettering themselves and expanding their knowledge base throughout their lifetimes. Valuing personal growth does not ensure success, but it does assist in keeping the brain active and resilient. It also increases the amount of resources you have available to you.

On the other hand, the culture and pace of today encourages people to be distracted and occupied all the time. A lot of people fritter away their spare time participating in activities that aren't productive, such as social networking, watching movies on YouTube, playing online games, and so on. Change agents with a positive mindset are less engaged in these kinds of activities and more concerned with their own personal growth. They put effort into bettering themselves so that they can devote more time to activities that bring them genuine pleasure, such as spending time with their families and making preparations for the future.

To make progress and experience change, you must first alter the way in which you carry out your daily activities. I have compiled a few suggestions to assist you in focusing on personal development, which may assist you in achieving your goals and improving your life in ways that you could not have envisioned:

Make education your top priority. A significant number of individuals hold the belief that receiving an education is critical to one's professional and personal growth. It has been established that expanding your knowledge can increase the flexibility of your brain, which is a fancy way of saying that learning is beneficial to your mental health.

You seem to have a successful career going, but is there anything else you could improve upon to move through the ranks? It's possible that your employer may be glad to find that you have an interest in gaining additional knowledge on subjects that will help you in your profession. Do you feel like your self-esteem could use a boost? Is this the right moment to pick up a guitar or another instrument? Alternatively, are you interested in enhancing your capacity to conserve money? (We are able to assist! It's possible that acquiring new skills that can help you enhance your life, finances, and profession won't be as challenging as you think it will be.

Spend some time learning about the topic by reading books, conducting research, and listening to podcasts.

Find a meaningful and pertinent volunteer activity that will enable you to learn more while also allowing you to assist others and meet your own needs at the same time.

To further your education, consider signing up for a course at a community college, taking private lessons, or attending an online academy.

Attend lectures and have conversations with people who are experts in the field.

You should be open to the idea of educating yourself on your own through a variety of different channels. Reading, listening to others, and engaging in conversation with others who have more knowledge than you do are all excellent ways to expand your horizons and acquire new information. Other abilities may require training, but if you're interested in developing them, the time and money you put in will be well worth it!

Acquire the skill of goal-setting

People who merely think about their goals in life, as opposed to writing them down, have a lower chance of achieving their goals than people who write them down and also think about them. The act of setting objectives for oneself serves as a form of motivation and provides something for one to work toward. Those who set actual goals for themselves report that the process makes it much simpler to accomplish their objectives. It is possible to further subdivide goals into more actionable steps, which will enable you to check off each step as it is accomplished.

Speak Up

Talk things through with a professional counselor or life coach. Changing your mentality is a process that requires patience and persistence. Before you can make a change, it's possible that you'll first need to confront the small voice in your head that is preventing you from moving forward. A good number of these beliefs begin to take shape when you are a youngster and continue to be reinforced throughout your life. If you work with a qualified life coach or counselor, they will be able to aid you in recognizing the limiting belief systems you hold, which will enable you to develop more quickly and effectively.

Learn to accept change

Because growth is impossible without change, it is important to explore how you respond to shifts in your environment. Your capacity for personal growth will be aided along the way by your acceptance of, and fortitude in the face of, change.

Try to take on more difficult tasks

To what extent may the activities you participate in contribute to your personal development? Is there a poetry reading event where you can gain some experience reading your work in front of an audience, such as an open mic night? Is there a group that caters to the new things you're interested in? Are you able to participate in the community band?

Find people and locations where you may connect with others in order to push yourself farther.

It is my sincere hope that these recommendations will be of assistance to you in locating ways to develop personally, spiritually, psychologically, and professionally in order to enhance your life.

Keep in mind that the drive to advance the process of growing as an individual is continuous. It requires making consistent investments in oneself by maintaining a high level of self-awareness, identifying areas of one's life that have room for improvement, and taking steps to realize those improvements. It is possible to include both soft and technical talents in this area.

You will gain a sense of direction, improved focus and effectiveness, increased motivation, and resilience as a result of being on a journey toward personal development. This will be in addition to the increased self-awareness you will experience. Even though the majority of the foundations are instilled in us at an early age, there is always more that can be learnt and improved upon in order for a person to become a better version of themselves.

Conquer your fears

Your capacity for development and advancement might be stifled by fear. If you have a fear of public speaking, for instance, you might want to enroll in a course or join a club that teaches individuals how to become better public speakers. If you lack the confidence to take chances, seek a guide who can assist you in making sound choices and help you develop your self-esteem. If you want to learn and grow, you should engage in activities that make you uncomfortable. If you are shy, you could try striking up a conversation with a stranger or introducing yourself to new people at a reception or workshop.

Read

Reading can not only increase the size of your knowledge and vocabulary but also keep you up-to-date on current events. It has the potential to boost your analytical and critical thinking skills while also stimulating your mind. You should make it a goal to read one chapter every day that is either instructive or inspiring, or one book per month.

Learn something completely new

Discover a new talent or field of study, either on your own or by enrolling in a course. You may, for instance, sign up for lessons to learn how to write in a more creative manner, how to use a different software program, or how to speak another language. Think about signing up for a webinar on a topic related to professional growth, such as starting a business or promoting your brand on social media. Make a request for comments. Approach a member of your family, a close friend, a work associate, or your manager and ask for their opinion on a recent endeavor or accomplishment. Make use of their constructive criticism as well as their favorable feedback in order to pinpoint problem areas. To acquire a new point of view, it is often necessary to seek the objective point of view of a third party. Observe the behaviors others exhibit and learn from them. Learn from those who motivate you by watching them and taking notes. This individual might be someone you know, such as a superior, a member of your own family, or a well-known public figure. Determine the qualities that you admire most in them and work to develop those same qualities in yourself.

Network

By connecting with a wide range of people, you can gain exposure to new concepts and gain an understanding of how to communicate and collaborate well with a variety of personality types. You will have the opportunity to interact with new individuals and cultivate connections that will prove useful in the years to come. Attend conferences and events centered on subjects that pique your interest or network through the various organizations that are associated with your industry or common interests.

Maintain a journal

You can become more self-aware and reflect on previous experiences, decisions, and discussions by writing in a diary on a daily or weekly basis, which can help you become more self-aware. It is possible to utilize it to organize and monitor one's goals and progress.

Meditate

Meditation is practised by a lot of individuals for the purpose of gaining clarity and consciousness, as well as relieving tension and anxiety. The practice of meditation can help you focus on aspects of your own growth and goals in a way that is more constructive, upbeat, and at ease. Even something as simple as arranging some time for yourself or taking a break from your work will help you relax and concentrate better.

Find a mentor, teacher or guide

If you are having trouble determining how to increase your self-development skills, you should discuss the issue with a mentor. It's possible that this person is a manager, a professor, someone you look up to, or even a professional personal development mentor.

CHAPTER 2

Reset Your Thoughts

People often argue that having information is the key to having power. As a result of your extensive knowledge, you have the ability to find success in situations in which others see none. Since there are constantly new things to learn as time goes on, there is no destination on the path that leads to enlightenment that can be considered to have been definitively reached. Learning is a never-ending process, but paying careful attention to the information that you acquire enables you to grow in enlightenment. Too frequently, we spend so much time trying to deny the reality of the situation that we miss the opportunity to retrain our brains to accept the reality for what it actually is. To unlearn means to relinquish knowledge or the understanding that it has become out-of-date for any reason, whether it be the discovery of the truth, the adoption of a new policy, or any number of other factors.

LEARN TO UNLEARN SO THAT YOU CAN RELEARN

On the other hand, to "relearn" something implies taking in new information that will help you and the environment around you become better. Relearning isn't always easy, but it's necessary if you want to be successful in achieving your goals. This is because it's difficult to let go of what you've thought to be the real thing for such a long time, which also makes it difficult to let go of what you've believed to be the real thing for such a long time. My experience has shown me that extremists are famously difficult to convince for the simple reason that their closed-minded worldview leads them to believe that their particular body of knowledge is the only one that could exist. "The illiterate of the 21st century will not be people who are unable to read and write; rather, they will be those who are unable to acquire, unlearn, and relearn (new information)" - Alvin Toffler. There can be moments when the things that we hold in such high regard might not be as precious as we thought they were. The fact of the matter is that there are layers that you might not ever be able to reach unless you go through some kind of mental retraining. If you don't give yourself permission to think positively and be open to new ideas, you might never get to the point where your mind is regenerated to the point where it's clear to everyone around you.

To summarize, we all have some comprehension of what it is that I am trying to say. We grow as individuals when we are willing to set aside our egos and make an effort to connect with and learn from anyone we can. This is essential to our development. It is always possible to learn something new, even if the source of the information is an idiot. Becoming an expert in something is a taught ability that anyone can achieve, just like becoming an expert in anything else. Nobody is born knowing how to be a lawyer; to successfully represent clients in court, one must first complete a substantial amount of schooling and work their way up through the ranks of the legal profession.

To become a physician, one must devote a significant amount of time and energy, but this is not a skill that is innately possessed by any human being. Considering that nobody else has anything to contribute, I could go on and on forever. No one else has anything of value to say. Even the people who are currently the ones you look up to the most have a history of learning that is visible to you, and that history of learning continues to be an important part of what makes those people so remarkable today. You won't be wasting your time if you learn anything because once you have information, it's impossible to get rid of it. One must never, under any circumstances, presume that a person's current circumstances are the consequences of their intrinsic aptitude or good fortune. No! You'll be amazed at the long-term benefits of giving your time to something worthwhile, and people become who they are as a direct result of how they've spent their time. People become what they are as a direct result of how they've spent their time. Because every one of us is the total of the decisions that we've made throughout our lives, it's critical to make decisions that are founded in logic.

You are completely unaware of how little information you possess. If you want to enter a certain industry but do not have the necessary background knowledge, you will need to devote time and effort to acquiring it before you can be considered an expert in that industry. No amount of wishful thinking will ever make you an expert in a subject you haven't studied.

Your lack of knowledge makes you appear more foolish than you are. The breadth of knowledge suggests that you cannot expect to excel at everything, but you can hone your talents to become an expert in the sector that you have chosen. Your outstanding delivery is yet another example of the exceptional quality of your work. One of the most common barriers to learning today is an individual's inability to put aside his or her ego and pride. Some people have an exaggerated sense of their importance, which prevents them from being harsh with others. Once upon a time, a wise man said, "Intelligent people learn from everything, everyone, and even fools," which sounded very strange given the fact that what does a fool have to offer? After that, I realized that one of the best ways to avoid becoming a fool is to observe and learn from others who are fools. There is some truth to be gleaned from that tone of sarcasm, even though it may come off as flip. According to the Bible, the children of Israel were going extinct as a direct result of their lack of education; consequently, receiving a proper education is critical for everyone. The reality is that you are limited in what you can accomplish with such a small amount of information, and as I've mentioned before, having more information enables you to take advantage of more opportunities.

YOU MAY NOT BE AWARE OF IT, BUT A PORTION OF YOUR SELF IS HUNGRY FOR FUTURE CHANGE

As a result of this, you must change the facets of your personality that contribute to your unhappiness. It is imperative that you make the necessary adjustments to the aspects of your life that will contribute to your success. If you've been dealing with something for a while that isn't producing the desired results, you should try shaking things up a bit. Change has the potential to bring amazing things to those who have been patiently waiting for them for years.

The following are some of the aspects that could benefit from some modification:

Changing one's perspective from one of self-consciousness to one of assurance. If you've been walking around with the wrong mentality about the things that happen in life, or if your personality just doesn't seem to mesh with the personalities of those around you, it might be time for a change. Do not give your poor reputation another chance to hurt you; it has already brought you more anguish than you can bear.

Change your surrounding environment and surround yourself with people who will motivate both you and your work.

As a general guideline, you should try to avoid associating with people who do not respect you. It is not the most important thing to do in life to compete for the approval of your contemporaries. There are other things that deserve your attention. Find new friends and keep looking until you find people who value and elevate you as a person. This is something you should do if the people you're hanging out with aren't conducive to the goals and plans you have for yourself.

Changes in work ethic have occurred, and many young people in today's society are lazy on the job. It's possible that hearing this will make you laugh, but in this day and age of digital advancement, your services can't be delivered inefficiently. If you're going to act like a slug, you can't expect to put food on the table. Do not allow yourself to fall into a routine of inactivity; instead, force yourself to get up and engage in some kind of activity.

THE MIND OF GOLD AS A GIFT: Unleashing Your Inbuilt Potential For Excellence

The gift of the golden brain is essential to understanding all that's going on. You are the center of attention, and I am the pivot point in this scenario. It's a divine scheme, and the two of us are the plan's most important cogs in the wheel. The divine operation that is the gift that lies within you can only be activated by you, as you are the one in command.

You already possess the skills necessary to create gold, which makes you the creator of your unique gift. To bring about the outcomes you desire, it is necessary for you, the divine core, to exercise control over this gold. When you create something, the most important tool you use is your imagination. You are the one who is driving, but you have no idea where you are going to take the precious gold mind. To bring about the outcomes you desire, it is necessary for you, the divine core, to exercise control over this gold. You can't go somewhere new with that golden intellect of yours since you haven't been there before. If you have a mind of gold, you have an infinite capacity for original thought and expression.

It is impossible to create something that you have absolutely no interest in creating. What you focus on grows to the point that you experience it as a tangible reality. If you have a mind of gold, you have the ability to create thought substance to back up the beliefs you hold. You could think that the thing you want is impossible to get, but if you keep your faith strong, you can make it happen.

This is how one can make one's aspirations become a reality. Therefore, adopting the mentality of gold is the means by which one can ensure his or her success, prosperity, and good health.

You serve as a hub for people's thoughts and ideas. Utilize the maximum extent of your intellectual capacity so that you can express everything that is already contained inside you. You can bring your thoughts to fruition with the assistance of the gold mind, which will enable you to expand and progress onto a more advanced level of existence.

We should not allow our thoughts to lull us to sleep, but rather let them serve as a source of inspiration for our originality. The process of creation is analogous to rousing oneself from sleep. When you create something, you awaken a part of yourself that you had assumed you already were. This is because you are the divine core and the expression of all creation.

Your golden intellect was bestowed upon you by God for a specific purpose, and it is now up to you to put that gift to good use. God does not want you to be selfish with this blessing; rather, He wants you to share it with others. Because it was provided to you, you ought to make the most of the opportunity it presents. As a result, you should make use of it so that you can improve and advance.

WHAT WE THINK, HOW WE FEEL, AND WHAT WE DO ARE ALL RELATED TO ONE ANOTHER

You need to completely submerge yourself in the mind and spirit of the subject matter of the work you are doing since thoughts are both concrete and obvious. Your skill has been bestowed upon you so that you may contribute your ideas, emotions, and actions to the creation that you have helped bring into existence. Because it is the law, you are responsible for your thoughts, feelings, and actions at all times. Once you have unearthed the gold that lies within you, you can begin to live by these rules. Bringing into existence what you desire requires you to connect with your spiritual side and direct your energy in that direction. The first step in the creative process takes place within. You are solely responsible for all of your successes. The substance of your works is whatever it is that you conceive into existence and bring into being.

Because God gave us a brain that can process ideas and use them to grow our spirit, we have the ability to be inventive. We advance as a result of the creative efforts we put forth, and as we grow, we realize that we, ourselves, are the primary impetus behind everything that we accomplish. Since you have endowed us with the capacity to think, feel, and act, permit us to put your skills to use in exercising those faculties that you have bestowed upon us.

You should direct your efforts toward the things that you want and deserve since you are wonderful, desirable, loving, creative, and talented. Your skills need to be pushed further, and you should not be afraid to reveal your true self.

You have been blessed with a mind made of gold, which is the divine nerve center from which an infinite number of possibilities can emerge. There is a priceless treasure lying dormant deep within you, just waiting for the right moment to emerge. When you put this gift to use, whatever you can think of has the potential to become a tangible reality simply through the power of thought alone. Once you step foot in this area, you have effectively entered the divine nerve center. At the very center of everything lies a hidden power source that must be protected at all costs. The process of creation, the synthesis of one's thoughts, emotions, and actions, is where the unspoken strength originates. This is the source of the strength that cannot be spoken of that everything you've created is centered on you as the creator. For this very reason, God endowed each of us with a brilliant intellect. When we decide what we want to produce from the center of divine operation when we love what we want to make, and when we create what we love we enter the center of all operations. When we love what we want to make, and when we create what we love, we enter the center of all operations.

You are aware that you alone are accountable for your thoughts; hence, you won't be able to relax until you have developed your very own seed of thinking, which is the gift that the gold mind bestows on its possessor. You are the king or queen of your creation; you are the king or queen of your own life; therefore, enter into the spirit of it, guide the divine center, and be the king or queen of your own life. You are the deserving, loving, and creative king or queen of your own life.

YOUR MENTAL STRENGTHS

It might sound like I'm talking about magic, but that's not the case at all. The term "mental power" is being used here to refer to a person's cognitive faculties. What kind of control do you have over your thoughts? Your way of thinking is one of the most powerful tools in your arsenal. Having this information is the first step toward channeling your strength in a beneficial way, and you should take it seriously. Simply using your mind can enable you to accomplish incredible feats.

The term "mental powers" should not be confused with "mental abilities," as the former is significantly more potent and remarkable than the latter. This category encompasses a wide range of psychic skills, including telepathy, mind control, mind reading, and the ability to manipulate dreams. The thing that I refer to as "mental power" is essentially a blessing bestowed by God.

The inner workings of the mind are what make up psychic powers. I am the central point of my business, which means that I am also the central point of my business. A power that can manifest itself in the material world is latent within each of us; this power is the power of thought. When you put in the work, success, and riches will come back to you in spades. How you have educated your mind to believe is the critical factor in determining whether or not you will be freed from depression.

The caliber of your thoughts determines the extent to which your mind can do things. You are exactly the person you imagine yourself to be. You have become whatever has predominated in your thoughts to the same degree that you have become that thing. If it's awful, you can still use the power of your intellect to become the person you were always meant to be, but if it's wonderful, that's fantastic. You have a reasonable brain because

God has provided you with one; utilize it to do good. A strong thought has the potential to have a significant influence, whereas a weak concept has absolutely no effect at all.

In a school atmosphere, you won't acquire the knowledge necessary to discover how to make use of your latent gifts. To be honest, I was one of those people who, like the rest of us, had no idea how much my mind was capable of until I discovered it for myself. Because we are humans, we are hardwired to rely on our five bodily senses of sight, hearing, smell, and taste to unearth the buried treasures that lie within. We smell with our noses, taste with our tongues, and touch with our skin. Our eyes allow us to see; our ears allow us to hear; our tongue allows us to taste; and our skin allows us to touch. Our environment, our concerns, and our conditions—what we see every day and how we react with our emotions—are the tools that we use to communicate with the outside world. Therefore, I had no idea that I possessed such tremendous powers until I started learning about the mind. Once more, the mind is an extraordinarily powerful tool, but you must learn to regulate it constructively and acceptably.

When I think about it, it baffles me why some people choose to end their own lives. They certainly suffer from depression. This is a result of the detrimental situations that they have had to endure. A major tragedy is caused by suicide. According to estimates provided by the World Health Organization (WHO) and the Global Burden of Disease study, almost 800,000 people take their own lives each year. In light of these findings, I have come to understand that suicide is not an option. Okay, they just want to put an end to everything. Is that a possible answer? When you even consider ending your life by taking your own life, you are admitting defeat to yourself. It's time to speak up. OPEN UP because sometimes it's ok that you're not ok. . You don't even know who you are, let alone the treasure you contain, which you need to find out about and let loose. Because you still have unrealized potential, you should never consider ending your life by suicide. It is not abnormal to run into difficulties. You cannot survive in this world without encountering difficulties, but you already possess the resources necessary to triumph over the difficulties you experience; all you need to do is search inward to unearth that wealth.

There is something to be said about pride. It is your perception of yourself. You are under its control at this point. It prevents you from moving away from the spot where you feel the most secure. I warn you: your safety is not guaranteed there. You are confined; your options are restricted. It is a form of self-sufficiency that will not make you aware of what you are capable of, and as a result, you continue to live in the "safe spot" since the ego is keeping you there. The ego is so possessive of you that it won't let go of you until you wake up and realize that you are living in misery and have no direction in life. The ego is so possessive of you that it won't let go of you until you wake up. You can be liberated from your ego if you are willing to receive the love that God has for you. Because your ego prevents you from showing love to others, the love of God is opposed to your ego. God cannot be found in a place occupied by the ego. In other words, the ego is a darkness that surrounds you, and until you see that light, you will continue to live in complete ignorance. Until you do see that light, however, you will continue to be ignorant.

Your environment shapes not only your ideas and behaviors but also your self-image and your beliefs. Your surroundings, including the people and objects in them, make up what is known as your environment. Your family, your friends, and your teachers, as well as what you watch and read, are all examples of this. You have an emotional response to the things that people say to you as well as the conditions of the objects that are in your environment. For instance, a teacher may tell a child that he is a loser because he is unable to keep up with the rest of the class. This child will undoubtedly go through life considering himself a disappointment. Because he has been conditioned to believe that he is a failure and cannot learn, he may even give up trying to improve himself academically. This is what he has been conditioned to believe, and until he understands that this is a massive hoax and until he becomes conscious of who he truly is, he will continue to be confined inside the cage.

A fact sheet compiled by education indicators and published in January 2015 provided insight into the competencies that young people achieve upon completion of their formal education. According to the fact sheet, the skills that youths acquire at the end of their formal education are partially a reflection of the career plans and accompanying program choices that they have made throughout their education. These decisions were made while the youths were in school. The importance that parents place on postsecondary education and the socioeconomic standing of their families is what drew my attention. According to the information provided in the fact sheet, "early consistency in career expectations was connected to the high parental value of postsecondary studies as well as high family socioeconomic status."

On the other hand, later consistency in professional aspirations was connected to earlier inconsistency in career expectations, as well as the low parental value of post-secondary degrees and lower family socioeconomic status. Therefore, the importance that a child's parents place on furthering their education beyond high school is directly proportional to the degree of consistency that the youngster exhibits in pursuing his or her career goals. That is the circumstance that the children were made to exist in; they were subjected to the influence of their parents. Imagine for a moment that a child wants to continue their education beyond high school but that his or her parents have doubts about it. Because this child has been conditioned by the skepticism of his parents toward postsecondary studies and perhaps the low family socioeconomic status, he may become disheartened and not be able to become what he is supposed to be. Additionally, this child's family may not have a high socioeconomic status. His parents' pessimistic outlook on further education has instilled in him the belief that he will never be able to pursue such an endeavor on his own. But he can if he truly wants to, and if he is desperate enough, then he will be able to look within himself and become conscious of his true identity, rather than the identity that his parents have given him. Then, he becomes aware of his abilities and asserts ownership over them.

What and who we listen to has a significant impact on the thoughts, beliefs, and actions that we have, as well as the picture that we create of ourselves. Unnecessarily, we are conditioned and programmed as a result of this. We are unable to be programmed, and we are unable to continue to be misled by the conditions that the outside world has imposed on us. However, when we become aware of the power that lies within us, we can understand that the outside world cannot control us but that we can control the outside world. If you have in the past been labeled a failure, once you realize the strength that lies inside you, you will no longer see yourself in that light and will not be affected by the sneers and jabs that you receive. You will be inspired to excel in all that you do and to conquer your fears of failing, ultimately removing the label that has been attached to you. You can look past the fact that you have low self-esteem, respect who you are, and believe in yourself even though you have low self-esteem. What came to pass? You have become aware of your abilities, both those that lie dormant within you as well as those that reside in your mind and were bestowed upon you by God.

God has a deep desire for you to uncover the capabilities of your mind. He has endowed you with mental powers that you must uncover and put to good use. You must have the willingness to explore this internal world to find your gifts because they are located in this internal realm. It is appalling that a lot of people live only by their senses because they are unaware of the potential that lies within them. It is because of this ignorance that a lot of people live their lives. They never do anything for themselves and spend their entire lives just listening to other people. Individuals like me and some other people are only able to uncover what we have within us, which is our powers, through the process of becoming aware of our surroundings.

As was discussed earlier in this chapter, the mind is a powerful tool; nevertheless, you have been given the ability to choose whether or not to accept information that is presented to the mind. When you have something to think about, you can dismiss the information, which is essential to the development of a golden mind. This is because the mind is meant for expansion, while the heart is meant for further expression. God wants you to grow, and he wants you to express yourself; he wants you to love and believe in yourself. He wants you to expand and express yourself.

It is up to you to build whatever you want. You have to have passion for what you make. If you don't have a strong emotional connection to what you're making, there's a good chance you're going about it all wrong and are confused. You have to have a solid understanding of what you want, be able to envision it, adore it, and then create it.

Consistency is necessary to create what you want. Inconsistency is a sign that one's mind is not very strong. It's possible that achieving what you want will take more time than you anticipate. However, the time you spend waiting helps you train your mind to be more patient. A consistent person is someone who is disciplined and who is able to accomplish his or her goals despite obstacles. What you once saw has been rendered invisible. Despite this, you continue to create, and you won't stop until your work is seen by others. It may take some time, but having patience and staying consistent will help you achieve your goal.

Building the life you want is a lot like putting up a house. In your head, you have a mental image of the kind of house you want to construct. Up until the point at which you begin construction, it will not be visible. Your perseverance is what makes the house visible, but as soon as you stop adding to it, it disappears into the ether. The site is still there, but construction has come to a halt. You will never be able to have the house of your dreams unless you get back into the construction business. You feel the same way about it. If you give in to the demands of the outer world and allow yourself to be trained and conditioned by them without being conscious of the strength that is inside, then that desire will die or be forgotten. This could result in remorse and unhappiness.

If you truly desire to accomplish that objective, you will put forth the effort necessary to do so. And while you are waiting for the goal to be accomplished, you will have the opportunity to become more self-conscious and aware of the significance of love, responsibility, and attitude. You place a high value on this objective, but you won't be able to accomplish it if you have the wrong mentality, and you won't be able to do it if you don't want it.

The golden mind is achieved when your ideas, feelings, and deeds are in harmony with one another. The intersection of your head and your heart can be found in your thoughts and feelings. You start to understand that you are able to awaken and that you do not have to remain dead on the inside as the head and the heart begins to come together. Before I became conscious of the gold mind, I was technically awake but dead on the inside; I had no sense of where I should go. But when I learned the power of imagination and the power of thinking most effectively, I came to life from the inside out. I also came to the realization that the center of creation is my mind and that the location where creation takes place is the thinking center. When you make something, you train your mind to think in specific ways. You have no influence over the outer world, but you do have power over the world within yourself, and you can do this by choosing whether or not to accept what comes into your mind. Your mind relies on you to develop and progress, and it also relies on you to bring about the creation that you desire.

Discovering your inner talents requires bravery, but once you do, you have the ability to produce the outcomes you desire. The greatest gift that God has given you is the ability to use your imagination. You have the ability to create anything you desire if you use your imagination.

Discover the power that lies dormant within you and put it to good use. The energies that are within you are rightfully yours to own. You only need to be conscious of it in order to gain your freedom and stop allowing yourself to be dominated by the outside world. The things that God has given you are riches that are found within you.

Your passion is the truth behind what it is that you wish to achieve. You permit yourself to fantasize about something, and then you make it happen. If you always have negative thoughts as a result of your interactions with the outside world, you will never be able to fulfill this desire. In this way, control is exercised over you. You are not claiming your powers as long as you continue to act in this manner. When you claim your powers, you unlock the ability to either acknowledge or dismiss whatever thoughts cross your mind. You make use of your abilities to create what it is that you want to create by thinking about it and achieving the result that you want to acquire.

When you rely solely on your senses for survival, you should prepare yourself to be followed. You have no idea how little knowledge you possess. You have been misled by both the programming that has been done to you and the conditioning that has been done to you. You have access to a means of self-creation and self-realization that enables you to bring about the outcomes you desire. This is accomplished by making use of God's gift of a golden mind.

Your mind is a place for creative and imaginative thinking. It is imperative that you make the most of this opportunity by making constructive use of your imagination. This was the purpose for which we were given the gift of the golden intellect. We have the power to alter our environments through the use of our imaginations. The only way to change one's circumstances is from the inside out, not from the outside in. You have to start believing in yourself before you can make use of the golden mind that God gave you. You are in command of your mind, which follows the directives that you give it.

When you tell your mind that you are accountable for your thoughts, feelings, and actions, you are communicating with your mind that you are in charge of it. Because you are a co-creator of your fate, you can shape the appropriate mentality as a consequence of this realization. Therefore, you need to keep a positive attitude because you are the one in command. You can either agree with or disagree with whatever thoughts enter your head. By exchanging your negative thoughts for positive ones, you can reclaim the power that was once held within your "golden mind." You are liberated from the yoke of servitude imposed upon you by the programming and conditioning imposed by the outside world.

Because their subconscious is in charge, even if they are awake, many people have the sensation that they are dead on the inside. If we want to avoid being ruled by our subconscious, we need to train our minds to think in the right way, and then we need to let go of our egos, otherwise, they will continue to get in the way. You have a responsibility to comprehend the fact that the ego was developed by another individual. Therefore, it is impossible for the ego to exist since you are employing the instrument provided by God, which is the gold mind. You just cannot afford to remain awake but dead on the inside because of the shift in the way you are thinking at this moment. You are envisioning a future filled with joy, health, and financial success. This is the authentic version of yourself, not the one that the outside world has conditioned you to believe you should be.

CHAPTER 3

Take Charge and Make Things Happen

You are responsible for both your life and your future; take charge of both. It is essential to remind yourself on a regular basis that you have the capacity to heal and maintain dominance over every aspect of your life. The ultimate litmus test of strength is the ability to persevere through adversity without giving in to despair. Being aware of your own power will prevent you from ever settling for being weak.

In spite of the fact that we are aware that this is not the case, it appears as if we have no control over the situation as a direct result of something that we have suppressed in our thoughts for such a long time that it is beginning to look as if we are truly powerless. Imagine something, and it will appear to your mind as if it were a reality even though it is only in your imagination. Because you start to believe the negative things about yourself that you tell yourself over and over again, it is essential to let go of any self-deprecating ideas you might have. Before you can physically step into it, your mind must first accept your power, your ideas must realign, and then you will become a reflection of it. Only after these steps have been completed can you physically step into it.

Your level of self-worth is inversely proportional to the quality of your thoughts; consequently, you should let go of any unfavorable beliefs you have about who you are. You need to retrain your mind so that it can accept the circumstances that will determine the course of your life. One's own thoughts are the wellspring from which all power flows. Because the thoughts you keep in your head become your experience of the world, it is important to cling to those that bring you joy.

Even though we have only a limited amount of control over the environment that we experience on the inside of our bodies, we can learn to become more mindful about the foods that we consume. Fear is a significant contributor to the fact that a large number of people, particularly young people, have a difficult time asserting their authority. Fear has a particular way of limiting one's potential that makes it unique. As a result of this, if you see other people making efforts to improve their future and the first thing that comes to your mind is the negative aspects of those efforts, you will begin to focus only on the negative aspects of those efforts, which will discourage others and limit the options available to you. The moment that concern enters the picture, forward motion comes to a grinding halt.

A few of the many reasons why you should avoid the letter F and the acronym it represents, "FEAR," are listed below.

Fear, as one of the most obvious aspects of its nature, makes it impossible for a person to attempt activities that they were previously capable of doing. It confines your thinking, forces you to stay in one place, restricts your mobility, and gradually but surely saps your strength until you eventually give up and feel like a failure. If you allow fear to take over, you will give up trying to improve your circumstances because you will convince yourself that there is nothing you can do to make things better. Imagine if you were to stifle your distinctive capabilities due to fear.

People I've met in my life have frequently said things like, "I know you to be prosperous; I used to have some of my own; at my young stage, I didn't settle for less, etc.; it's been part of me; I go all out irrespective of my query, "What happened?" The seeds of my fear were planted! It throws a wrench into your plans and makes them appear to be pointless, but in the end, you find out that taking that step was actually the best option.

Understanding that fear is nothing more than an illusion that your mind creates is one of the most important steps in conquering it.

It is possible to pass away from fear; I believe I just gave an example of how fear can kill more quickly than many diseases right now. Even though this mission has already been completed with success, the anxiety and subsequent high pressure that it causes are almost always counterproductive. Certain individuals are prone to experiencing anxiety as a result of the nature of the future being unknown. As a result, they become stifled by this idea, and after clinging to it for a while, they begin to accept their permanent state of fear as normal. This idea has a negative effect on them.

Telling yourself that only the courageous and determined can accomplish great things is a great way to motivate yourself to work toward your goals. It is essential to maintain a pragmatic and optimistic attitude at all times, even if you reach a point in your life where you don't believe things can turn out the way you want them to. To step into your power, you need to believe in God and work on developing traits like courage, self-confidence, and independence from other people.

When those who look up to their mentors also respect the path they took, that is when you know you have arrived at the right conclusion about the nature of the relationship between the two. Because triumph over adversity is inextricably linked to accomplishment, it is appropriate to value both the accomplishment and the anguish that it brought about. There is no foolproof strategy that will guarantee victory.

Those who approach challenges with an "I can!" attitude serve as an inspiration to me. The implication of this statement is that you should never accept yourself as being below average. the mentality that one is always prepared for whatever may come their way, regardless of the circumstances.

Now is the time to seize the opportunity; do not waste it!

You shouldn't put off beginning to feel more confident until a particular day or time because you shouldn't wait for that.

The first day you make the conscious decision to emerge marks the beginning of your ascent to prominence.

There is no such thing as an inappropriately early time to assume a leadership role. Because of where we came from, it is your duty to come into this reality at any time to establish dominance, control territories, and subjugate others.

Do not beat yourself up for getting lost in thought during the day. You are the only person standing in the way of the accomplishment of your most audacious goals and objectives. Imagine yourself in the future, having already accomplished the most difficult objectives you set for yourself. Make use of your creativity; when you put what you've been thinking into action, you'll be amazed at the results.

A young African girl once bemoaned the fact that she has a croaky voice and expressed her desire to become a singer, but as time went on, the notion of becoming a singer eventually took over her life. One day, she came across a seasoned performer who provided her with some useful guidance. The performer told her, "If you really want to sing, start practicing right away, and don't quit along the way, even when you feel weak or intimidated by another." At first, I'm sure it seemed snarky to her because so many singers claim to have been born with their talent, so she couldn't possibly catch up to the competition by practicing as she was told to do. However, the first attempt, which was unsuccessful (as is customary), was made. She was so ashamed that she cried the entire way back to her house, and she made a solemn promise to herself that she would never again do anything that would bring such humiliation to herself in public. She could have worked on improving her appearance through practice, but instead she accepted the fact that "she isn't a good vocalist" and kept her appearance the same. After one year, her passion for singing was just as strong as it had ever been, so she gave it another shot, and just like the first time, things didn't turn out the way she had hoped they would. On the other hand, she returned this time with the full intention of accomplishing what she set out to do, and since then, she has put out some music that is absolutely breathtaking, establishing herself as one of the best singers that I am personally familiar with. If she had accepted the challenge when it was first presented to her, I have no doubt that she would have done just as well as she did this time around. As long as you are alive, the clock will never stop ticking, and it will always be your time. Although a lot of people will tell you that "it's not your time yet," the truth is that the clock is always ticking and it is always your time. As a result of your lack of readiness to seize the moment and make it your own, it gave the impression that this opportunity was never presented to you. Take advantage of every available opportunity because this is your time. No one should be allowed to use the justification that "it's not your time" in order to prevent you from making the most of the limited opportunities that are available.

PUT YOUR PLANS AND DREAMS INTO ACTION

Dreams do not have a will of their own and do not act solely on their own. If you want to see any of your dreams come true, you are going to have to put in some work. If you ever give up on your goals, those goals will eventually give up on you. So don't ever give up on them. Dreams are not unreachable aspirations; rather, they represent goals that are within one's grasp.

Nothing takes place unless it is caused by a driving force in some way. What steps are you taking to make sure that your goals will eventually become a reality? You simply need to keep moving forward until you have accomplished what you set out to do. If you don't start challenging yourself in new ways and learning new skills, you won't have any idea how much strength and power you possess. If you haven't yet taken the last step, you'll never know how much simpler it is to achieve your objectives, even though they may seem insurmountable. It unlocks the potential for strength that has been dormant within you all along.

When you tell yourself you have no chance of succeeding, everything else in your life starts to fall apart. Keep fighting; there is still a chance. Although many people indeed tell themselves that they'll achieve their goals "someday," the fact of the matter is that there's no better time than the present to get started on achieving those goals.

Participation in the appropriate activities is required to keep one's dreams alive. However, if these activities are not undertaken, the dream will eventually become dormant. You'll be glad that you made it a daily goal to accomplish your objectives and to increase your influence and authority in the future.

CHAPTER 4

We were Created to be Unique and Unusual

Being one of a kind means distinguishing oneself from the rest of the pack. Sometimes the thoughts, activities, or desires that we have won't be shared by other individuals. Being one of a kind and set apart from everyone and everything else is the same as being unique or peculiar. Everyone exudes their distinct energy, and this is what determines their worldview and the things that are most important to them in life. The idea that you can influence another person's behavior or thoughts to be more similar to your own may seem absurd. This is because of the haphazard way in which our brains are wired. When it comes to a critical juncture in our lives, the realization that each of us is unique and special in our way can be a game changer. Be conscious of the fact that we are blocking your line of sight. You have to be comfortable with the idea that you are distinct from everyone else.

One of the things that take place on our planet is what we call "variety." Every single person has his/her own set of distinguishing qualities. The idea that we can be brought together against our will in the same space is not only doomed to failure but also grossly misleading. Our individual peculiarities and eccentricities are more likely to be kept at the "unconscious" or "subconscious" level rather than making their way into our conscious awareness. We have progressed to such a degree in the labyrinth of social confusion. Many people are unable to recognize the distinctive features that are exclusive to them since other people have such a fascinating effect on them. It is essential, in my view, to emphasize the one-of-a-kind characteristics that each of us possesses. It is impossible to stress the importance of having a healthy sense of self-awareness and self-consciousness. You can only infuse your very fibers with renewed vigor if you accept the fact that you are a unique individual.

Have you ever given any thought to the idea that you might be exceptional or peculiar in some way? Many individuals have not yet completed their metamorphosis because they have never posed this penetrating question to themselves. This is the primary reason for this.

You may need someone to point out to you how to get out of the "unconscious" mindset that's been keeping you from recognizing your individuality. You see, for us to bring about the change that we want, we need to teach ourselves to think carefully and to meditate on who we are as individuals.

ASSUME AND CULTIVATE A VARIETY

That feeling of being different and alienated from others around you; it is possible for it to be annoying, uneasy, and even frightening. It has the potential to isolate you by making you believe that everyone else is in possession of a vitally significant secret while you are the only one who is unaware of its contents. Is it true that being different automatically qualifies one for exclusion, although this is the way our lives were intended to be lived?

As I mentioned earlier, this school lacked the essential structures that are required for a school. As a consequence of this, I will claim that they were lacking in terms of offering necessary amenities for students as a whole, even though they were widely considered to have excellent academic programs. The fact that our professors held advanced degrees like master's degrees and doctorates and had a wealth of knowledge contributed to the school's reputation of excellence in the community.

When I was a student at Phwezi Boys' Secondary School, I had the opportunity to speak with one of the school's directors, Hon. Chipimpha Mughogho. He was also one of the school's founders, a politician of high caliber, and a member of parliament. He renovated the school and turned the isolated village into a town, which resulted in the creation of many employment opportunities in the community and lifted many people out of poverty.

We, as separate individuals, band together to create a community, a collective, and ultimately a society. We are not a mass-produced item but something that has been handcrafted. What does it matter then if we don't look, talk, or act like the people that are around us?

When I was younger, the things that Hon. Chipimpha Mughogho did serve as a source of motivation for me, and it became a goal of mine to be in a position where I could assist other people one day. He instilled in me an optimistic outlook on politics and the conviction that one person's efforts, directed at alleviating the plight of the masses, may make a difference and bring about positive change.

The thought that I may be of tremendous benefit to individuals and communities moved me to tears. I was confident that I would succeed; all that was required of me was dedication, concentration, and effort. In addition, I'd say that his actions and the way he went about performing his charity deeds aroused my interest in politics and inspired me to get involved. He was a devout follower of Christ, an elder in the church, and known as a man of the people due to the widespread esteem in which he was held. While he was in Malawi, he was a member of the "Central African Presbyterian" church. I started making contact with people in my sphere of influence. My political viewpoint was significantly shaped as a direct result of the book "Chipimpha Mughogho." Unfathomable was his approach to offering love to other people, and he contributed much to the betterment of his society. He was able to satisfy the bulk of the people's fundamental requirements. I would like to instill in young people the mentality that they should never give up and that they should be consistent in everything they do.

Surely, you are familiar with the terms "cultural shock" and "collision of cultures." Although humanity was intended to be full of nuanced differences, these things continue to occur. Even though we never intended to be carbon copies of one another, there are a great number of us who have lost the ability to see past our differences and accept them.

The variety of life on Earth is a reflection of how God created it. The New King James Version of the Holy Bible says in Acts 17:26, "And He has made every nation of mankind from one blood to dwell on all the faces of the globe, and He has fixed their assigned times and the borders of their homes." (NKJV)

Consider a world in which everyone and everything was always the same and there was no way to tell one from another. Even in this information-driven day and age, we are easily bored by our surroundings because we are subjected to so many different messages daily. The reason for this is that we are surrounded by so much information. Why therefore go to such great lengths to ensure that you "fit in?"

The fact that it is simpler to just blend in with the crowd is one explanation that may be considered. If something goes wrong or you make a mistake, you will have the option of hiding behind other people if you do not stand out from the crowd. Having said that, the issue that needs to be asked is, "Who made it an absolute reality that if a group of individuals shares the same opinion or behavioral pattern, then it is automatically the proper course to take?"

Consider the concept of being influenced by one's peers. In this context, "Peer Pressure" means the direct influence of individuals by colleagues or a person who is persuaded to follow colleagues by adjusting one's beliefs, values, or actions to align with those of the influential group or individual. Peer pressure can also happen when someone changes their thoughts, feelings, and actions to match those of their coworkers. Peer pressure can also be referred to as "social pressure."

Does achieving something like that sound like it would be worthwhile? Being forced to alter the person you are to meet the expectations of others? There are other topics that I believe need more of your attention, but this is not one of them. It is important to guard against allowing the acts of others to shape how you evaluate yourself. You shouldn't worry about fitting into the mold that has been created for you by other people's expectations. God has already determined what constitutes an acceptable standard, and he has given you a compass to help you navigate correctly. If you let yourself become preoccupied with fitting in by any means possible, you will divert your attention from the most essential duty you have yet to complete, which is to carry out the assignment that God has given you here on earth. You could say something along the lines of, "But it is also my obligation to interact with and live in harmony with others." In this particular respect, you are quite correct! Nevertheless, sharing your space with other people does not require you to give up your identity in the course of doing so. It is not your obligation to make other people feel comfortable in your presence if they are unable to do so since you are "different." It is up to you to behave in a way that is fitting for the one-of-a-kind and exceptional individual that God designed you to be.

Outstanding people require a unique grace, while those who are just ordinary can be ordinary. Because you were not created to be like everyone else, you should immediately start embracing and expressing your individuality. I have decisively discussed some tips on how to get started on that road in my book, "Mindset of Greatness: Master Your Life and Switch from Lack to Limitless." If you are on a quest to master the art of greatness, it's expedient that you get it.

> Reflecting on your original self every individual has their own unique perspective on the world, which is mostly shaped by the experiences they have had and the paths they have taken in life. No one will choose the same paths for their lives as you do. Every successful and unsuccessful event, every moment of strength and weakness, every moment of triumph and

failure, and every piece of knowledge and wisdom you obtain are directly proportional to your willingness to accept, learn from, and think creatively outside the box. In a world where so many people feign illusional versions of themselves, it's an incredible feeling to know that you are an authentic one, the only one of your type. Simply expressing your personality in a way that is authentic to you is the most effective way to do so. If you want to experience the life that was meant for you, you need to detach yourself from the crowd and project a new image of yourself to the world. Devise a moment when you can speak with your inner self without disturbance. There is a truism that "the best teacher can only be found within." The moment you cast away any personality that has been hoisted on you by society, your sense of confidence will increase, and you will have an easier time dealing with the outside world. This can be achieved when you reflect on who you truly are. What is it that makes you different from others? What kind of difference do you want to make or live for that will make the creator proud of you? You might need to genuinely write your answers down. Just by reflecting on who you are, you will definitely make an impact that will be difficult for others to forget.

Respect your identity and privacy. Being original and distinct in the modern world has become increasingly difficult. The reason for the deficiency is that people hanker after gratifying the opinions of others at the expense of their identity. Many people don't want to face the oppressive reality that not everything we do will please them, and we are also not ready to put it in their faces. Besides, people who feel they are not good enough spend their entire lives emulating someone else in the mistaken belief that they are not good enough themselves. One of the components of this is realizing and being okay with the fact that not everyone will be happy for you. Because of this, there will always be someone who is more intelligent, wealthy, younger, and more gorgeous than you are. However, no one will ever be able to take your place. Always be true to who you are. If you truly want to make a difference in the world, you must make the conscious decision to remain grounded in reality. Do not make the mistake of trying to emulate others. Have a good time being yourself! Therein is the source of your greatest potential for power. If you want people to take you seriously as an individual, you have to be willing to go it alone. However, this is the very place where your uniqueness may blossom.

Who is the brain behind your fate? "There is no other path for you to take in life than to become the person you desire to be." The idea that you are the master of your own fate is emphasized in the phrase above. This is something that each and every one of us needs to keep at the forefront of our minds on a daily basis. To begin, it is impossible to experience genuine joy if one does not first recognize and accept who they are in this world. Understanding both your capabilities and your limitations is necessary in order to fully embrace your identity. When you are concerned about the judgments of other people, it can be scary to embrace the unique qualities that make you who you are. Being one of a kind is more valuable than achieving perfection. After all, not a single person is faultless. The fact that we all have our shortcomings is not always a negative trait. Our imperfections are what set us apart from other animals and give each of us a one-of-a-kind personality. Imagine how dreadful the world would be if everyone were flawless. It would be a really dull experience. It can be challenging to accept yourself as you are. Nevertheless, it is the establishment of your own personality once you have fully embraced it.

Discover your creative side. Being unique gives you the feeling that your life has meaning and purpose. Our uniqueness may be seen in the things that we enjoy doing, the creativity that we express, the thoughts that we have, the values that we hold, and even in the way that we present ourselves to the outside world on a daily basis. Recognize and celebrate the qualities and skills that set you apart from everyone else in the world. Being unique is the final key to happiness. Every person possesses their own unique creative gifts, which are shaped by the perspective that they bring to their work.

If you want to develop into a better person, you need to work on improving the skills you already have.

Be sincere and honest with others, rather than pretending to be someone else.

Never be hesitant to display your talents and qualities in front of others.

Your opinions are important to us.

Opinions shouldn't be allowed to divert your attention.

Explore uncharted territory by challenging yourself with novel experiences.

Recognize and accept your shortcomings, and take on the challenges you confront.

You should constantly remind yourself of good things by saying positive affirmations.

Never, ever, ever compare yourself to anyone else, especially not yourself. Creating is the goal.

Have faith in the path you have chosen.

Even with all of your shortcomings, the world needs you. You are free to live your life in the most fulfilling way that is feasible for you, so long as the way you live your life doesn't hurt anyone else. It's a great feeling to know that you're the only one of your kind. However, in order to be successful in that endeavor, you need to be a real, genuine, and genuine individual. Recognize and embrace the uniqueness that you possess. It is essential to have this understanding because you will never be able to satisfy your own needs if you spend all of your time trying to fulfill the needs of others. In addition, if you want to make a difference in the world, you have to be willing to fight for the things that you believe in. Take pleasure in everything — big and small — that contributes to just who you are in a broader sense. Your perspective has the potential to encourage others to accept who they are!

"

You shouldn't water down who you are
for anyone or anything.
You are sufficient! Be confident of who you are
and don't apologize for it.

– Allan Mandindi

"

CHAPTER 5

REFINE YOUR ROUGH DIAMOND

Gold is not admirable in its natural state. It needs to go through a difficult procedure to become alluring. You must fight to become someone better than you were before coming to this planet. You must refine yourself.

Someone may have told you something along the lines of, "My ultimate dream is to be normal." Nobody I know is born with the intention of having a mediocre life or accomplishing nothing significant in their lifetime. If you're anything like me, you want to differentiate yourself from the crowd, be one of a kind, and perform at the highest possible level.

That is another one of God's hopes and dreams for you. He never engages in random or aimless behavior in any way. Everything has been carefully prepared for it. He was responsible for determining our physical characteristics, our personalities, our ancestry, as well as our intelligence. This indicates that there is something specific that God wants you to achieve in your current form, making use of the skills that make up your unique combination. It is possible that it will take some time for you to discover what it is, to mature into that person, and to be entirely at ease with your identity.

I am well acquainted with the route that I will take. For me, the battle to acknowledge and embrace what makes me special started at a very young age. It's possible that it's due to the fact that when I was a little child, I had to study for my final primary school leaving examinations when I was left alone in a rural school in Lilongwe, Kasiya, named "Kamzimbi." This was due to the casual demeanour I had at the school I attended before this one in the city.

My thought process had to be completely reorganized after moving because I had moved to an environment that was not conducive to learning. The institution had a stellar reputation for achieving outstanding achievements, yet it did not have the requisite facilities of a contemporary educational institution. This area did not have any conveniences such as a library, clean restrooms, desks and seats for students to sit on, hostels, and other such facilities. I was left alone for a full school year, yet the influence that the school had on me will be with me for the rest of my life.

When I was a kid growing up in Malawi, my dad was always quite successful in school. He comes from a family that has a long tradition of success in education.

During his time period, getting accepted into the university was a difficult task because the standards for admission were quite high and only exceptional candidates were able to succeed in the screening procedure. One of the most notable participants was my father. Due to the uncanny intelligence he possessed, he was accepted to the University of Malawi and went there to pursue his education. After that, he worked his way up through the ranks of the Malawi Civil Service, where he was highly regarded.

Even though my mother was a primary school teacher, I had a difficult time in primary school because I did not take my academics seriously. This caused my father a great deal of frustration because he wanted me to be just like him. My mother was a primary school teacher.

It's possible that members of my family will make fun of me because I couldn't get it together. Despite this, there was a certain quality that distinguished me from others. I found out at a young age that I was blessed with a mind that retained everything I learned very well. This gift has helped me advance and not fail any examinations, albeit not to the standard that my father expected of me. I have been blessed with a mind that retains everything I learn very well. As a consequence of this, my father made the decision to relocate me to the hamlet where he was raised for the duration of one year in order to develop a more serious attitude in me towards my academics.

Because of the area's isolation, there was no power or any of the other conveniences that I was accustomed to having at my former home. My mind was racing with dark thoughts, and I was certain that my parents were hostile to me and that they had left me to suffer as a result of their decision. I was heartbroken and crestfallen. I went with my best buddy, who found himself in the same predicament I was wallowing in. Because none of us was very engaged in our studies, our parents came to the conclusion that it would be beneficial for us to travel there together in order to gain some perspective on life.

When we arrived, the head teacher greeted us and informed us that we were the school's first students from the city.

At this moment in my life, I had no idea where this was going to lead me. But all that kept going through my head was how my hopes and ambitions for achievement had been shattered. Although the school was good and produced good results, there was no one that I could look up to as a role model or who had gone through the school and achieved greatness at the time. There was also no one that I could look up to as a graduate of the school who had achieved greatness at the time.

I had the impression that this was the last possible step. I could not for the life of me fathom that anything positive could come from this experience, nor did I have any idea that it would prove to be the most critical juncture in my life.

Everyone will face trials and tribulations in life that will put our faith in God to the test. Have faith and never give up; the obstacles we face in life are put there to help us mature or restart our lives; all we need to do is persevere through them. We have to be able to view the experience of being rejected as a constructive opportunity that paves the way for fresh beginnings in our lives.

I was able to pay more attention to my inner self as a direct result of the education I received at that school. As a consequence of this, I became aware that there was more to my life than what I was experiencing at the time.

Initially, because of the isolated setting I was in, I became a shadow of myself. However, as time went on, I realized that there was a natural gift in me that needed to be nurtured, and all I needed to do was stay focused on what I was doing. I was able to come to this realization as a result of the passage of time.

The more time I spent at 'KAMZIMBI,' the more I noticed a change taking place inside of me. I came to appreciate people regardless of where they came from or what their social standing was. A new version of myself formed, and people started confiding in me to such an extent that I made the decision to fulfill the expectations that other people had of me while also focusing on improving myself to become more reliable. I evolved into someone who is more patient, always willing to provide a helping hand, sensitive, and responsive to the needs of others. But none of this transpired until I came to terms with the circumstance I found myself in. The most significant barriers we face almost always result from our refusal to acknowledge the truth about our circumstances. You won't be able to make a change unless you come to terms with your reality, and when I finally did that, I saw the beginning of my transformation.

I graduated from secondary school in 2002 with high grades, but I was unable to enroll at the University of Malawi since there were such a huge number of pupils who achieved a perfect score. When I tried to find a way out of the situation, it was yet another frustrating experience for me. An opportunity to work with the Malawi National Intelligence Bureau has been presented to me. This was my one and only opportunity to enter the state service and get over the disappointment of not getting accepted to the University of Malawi. I was very disappointed that I was not selected for the role. Despite the numerous setbacks and mistakes that occurred during this time in my life, I refused to surrender and give up. I decided to check into other potential avenues instead.

I was offered the chance to study accounting in the United Kingdom (UK) in 2003, something I later dropped after I realized that it was not the route I wanted to take in terms of my professional life. Keeping one's composure through such a trying year was not as simple as it may appear now, but I had thought that with a lot of effort and perseverance, the stars would be the starting point for my journey.

Fast forward to 2008, when I made a choice that would transform the course of the rest of my life: I enlisted in the British Army. I was chosen to join the Royal Logistics Corps, and that's where I got my military training.

After finishing my initial basic training at Army Training Regiment Bassingbourn, which is located in the south of England, I was sent to the British Army Logistics School in Deepcut for specialist training, where I was given the opportunity to get trained as a logistics supplier specialist. After graduating in 2011, I was immediately sent to my first conflict assignment in Afghanistan. There, I served a 6-month tour of duty before being awarded the "Her Majesty's Medal of Service," which was like having a dream come true. After returning home, I was presented with the medal, which was a dream come true. What if I had given up because I felt like I had wasted so many years?

Along the path, there will be many obstacles, many reasons to give up, and many frustrating moments; yet, if you have patience and determination, you will be successful.

Because I was able to endure through the challenges, I no longer have to battle as much as I did in the past.

Everyone you come across out there has the makings of a great person somewhere down the line. There is no one who is too restricted to achieve greatness; the only thing that may hold somebody back is their thinking. What is the extent of your mental capabilities? Do you picture yourself becoming the next president of your country someday? Do you think you have what it takes to graduate as the student who has achieved the highest grade in your division? What is the extent of your mental capabilities? Do you want to reach your full potential?

"Greatness is a mentality that you have to bring with you everywhere you go." Professor Ebube's Psalm

You might not look like it right now, but if you believe in yourself and put in enough effort, you will eventually become it. People who are willing to have visions and put them into action are the ones who will be successful; success is not for those who are lazy.

No one is more fortunate than the other; what matters most is how you go about living your life today since that will define what comes out of it.
– Allan Mandindi

The decisions you make and the actions you take today will leave a blueprint for your future, and if you do not give the activities in your life the attention and priority they need right now, the consequences will become immediately apparent. What you make allowances for right now will become immediately clear.

It has come to my attention that a lot of people don't even have a clear idea of what they want out of life. This is extremely risky, as when you don't know what you want, everything looks like it could be it. Think about how you can embrace and take ownership of the "fate" of any life you find yourself in.

People who are determined do not take everything; rather, they are aware of what really belongs to them and how to acquire it.

The choices you make in life have the power to either positively or negatively affect the course of your future.

– Professor Psalm Ebube

There were times when I wanted to give up, much like myself in the show "Kasiya." However, as I realized that all I was doing was for my future, I was able to see that perseverance pays off in the end.

It didn't disturb me that I was lying on thatched ground, and the mice that scurried between my legs every night didn't distract me from my slumber either. On the other hand, I had significantly more compelling reasons to pursue my goals. I was confident that one day people from all over the world would hear my tale and that I would be a significant source of inspiration for a lot of people.

Perhaps the times I always dreamed happened because I believed in myself, which is something I continue to do today. You don't need the rest of the world to see what you're carrying; you don't need everyone to believe in who you want to be; all you'll ever need to become is someone who believes in themselves. You don't need anyone else to believe in who you want to be. "You are your first and only audience and supporter, so you have to have faith in yourself before anyone else will."

Everyone is capable of great things, but most young people aren't even aware of their own potential since the world around them is so full of distractions. Some younger individuals look for the easiest way to achieve success, despite the fact that this is almost never the case.

Every successful person you come across will have a tale to tell that will blow your mind and leave you speechless.

– Allan Mandindi

There will always be things to divert your attention, but if I was able to get through it, you certainly can as well.

Today, I could have chosen to be a nobody like everybody else does; we all have that option. During that time, I was confronted with difficulties in a wide range of domains. When I was a young lad, I remember feeling frustrated because I knew I should have been at the University of Malawi with my friends, but instead, I was forced to remain at home for a number of months because of the circumstances that I found myself in. During that particular period, the choice to continue being determined and relevant was one that I made on my own. You will eventually come to the conclusion that the only person who is capable of making the best decision for you is yourself. I vowed to do great things and to have a positive impact on the lives of others. What are your plans for the rest of the day?

What kinds of things pique your interest? Throughout the years that I spent researching and studying, I came to the conclusion that the majority of people who possess natural gifts are unaware of those gifts until they begin to focus more attention on themselves and their purpose.

Before I made the conscious decision to pay attention, I had no notion that I had the ability to both listen to and counsel other people. My father took me to that distant place in large part because of my sense of humor, which was one of the main reasons he took me there. He was well aware that my future would have been negatively impacted if I had continued in that direction. I had the sensation of being abandoned, but in the midst of everything, I was able to find myself. My first step was taken by my father when he drove me there, but the following steps have been taken by me because I am the one who must assume responsibility.

That "village" served as a learning environment for me, and my account wouldn't be complete if I didn't mention the once-isolated community that provided me with valuable insight into how to live my life. All of the daydreams that young people indulge in these days are insidiously depriving them of the capacity to engage in profound thought and the drive to accomplish more than they are now capable of.

If you don't act on the dreams you have right now,
they'll turn into nightmares in the future.

– Allan Mandindi's

Your attitude and character are crucial factors to consider when attempting to cultivate a mentality of excellence. I have always been the type of person who respects others and treats everyone fairly, regardless of their age, gender, or background. I believe this to be the best way to live. This kind of thinking has helped me become more successful in whatever circumstance I find myself in. When I was in elementary school, my teachers frequently gave me opportunities to act in a leadership capacity. When I got to the secondary school in Phwezi, everyone respected me because I gave them that respect.

My innate aptitude for leadership was beginning to come to the surface when I was given the position of prefect by the teaching staff. During the time when I was in basic training for the army, my fellow soldiers elected me to take on the role of leader until I graduated. At the university, I served as a course representative, which meant that I was responsible for advocating the interests of all of my fellow students before the university board and the administration of the institution. Across a wide variety of committees, I've held both the chair and vice chair positions. My perspective on things and the people I collaborate with determine everything that happens.

When you fixate incessantly on the things that are "wrong" with you, you draw attention away from the things that are "great" about you. No matter how put together we appear to be on the outside, we all face obstacles and challenges on the path to becoming the person we desperately want to be—the person God created us to be. Despite how put together we appear to be on the outside, My entire life has been dedicated to tearing down boundaries and encouraging people to hold onto hope no matter what. My experience has shown me that if we put our attention on this, God will assist us.

You need to be aware of what I call "Distinctly You Blockers" and then overcome them with "Distinctly You Builders" in order to thrive and be distinct in your uniqueness. I call these the "Distinctly You Blockers." Even though I don't pretend to know everything there is to know about them, I do feel that the things I've learned can help you stay in the race (or get back in it), get pumped up, and ultimately win. These are tried-and-true concepts that I've applied to my own life and found to be successful.

"Only those with truly outstanding minds possess the virtue of patience.

– Allan Mandindi's

CHAPTER 6

Engrain your Own Imprint on the Soil

Put yourself one step ahead of the rest of the people in the crowd. We are all part of the same large group of people. Even though we all have the same goal—to make our lives more meaningful by doing something beautiful—we almost never deviate from the path blazed by others. Following in the footsteps of others will never take you to stunning locations. Therefore, you need to pave your own way to achieve success in your life.

Don't let yourself be enslaved by the people. Acknowledge your value to the world and forge your own path. Gain an understanding of your own belongings as well as your identity and individuality. You stand out from the rest of the people. Create your own path, prevail over challenges, come to an understanding of who you are, and accept who you really are.

Feel proud of the unique person you are. You are not a duplicate of anyone else; you are an original. God has bestowed upon you a variety of qualities and attributes. Each person on this earth has a distinctive appearance and personality because God created them that way. Therefore, you should quit trying to be like other people and start being yourself. Bring the appropriate items and people into play. No matter how tall, short, fair, or dark you are, everyone deserves respect. There is a quality that sets you apart from others. Be aware of your worth. There is a reason God created you. When you are able to accept yourself just as God created you, you are bestowing a favour on yourself. Being unique and not fitting in with the crowd can be a blessing.

Put an end to comparing your life to that of other people. Don't let yourself become a fool by believing all that other people tell you. People will never stop judging. It is up to you to confront the unknowns and get control of your thoughts in order to embrace who you are. You tell a very different story than I did. Don't let society define who you are; instead, chart your own course and follow your own lead.

Do one of these things if you want to be a leader and set yourself apart from the rest of the crowd:

Believe in Yourself: Start believing in yourself. Learn as much as you can about yourself. Start behaving differently than other people by listening to what your soul tells you to do. Begin by acknowledging both your capabilities and your limitations. You have a greater understanding of yourself. Learn what is healthy for you, and model your behavior after that. Your life can be transformed by something as basic as a belief. You are the model for yourself to follow. Having faith in one's own capabilities is essential to achieving success in whatever endeavour one undertakes. Believe in yourself and have faith that you can succeed in spite of what other people think. Take steps in the direction of your goals and be consistent in doing so. Make a move, perform an activity, and so forth. Don't just sit and envision it. Take action, and don't allow your fear to hold you back. Conquer the wars, have faith, and believe in yourself so that you can make it to the end. There is no magic formula for success; all you need to do is convince yourself that what you're doing is exceptional.

Quit focusing more on negativity. Put a halt to it. There is no one more familiar with you than you are. You are completely familiar with all aspects of yourself. You are aware of all of your capabilities, whether they be strengths, weaknesses, or blunders. You are aware of the actions you need to take in order to accomplish your goals. It's simple to provide words of wisdom, but much more challenging to put them into practice. People will offer you guidance based on their experiences, but they won't know anything about your situation. Therefore, you should listen to your own counsel, which will help you discover your way. Get in the habit of listening to your intuition. You have a good understanding of your gut impulses. In that case, let's proceed. Have the courage to act on your instincts and your heart's desires. Confront peril and show courage in the face of adversity. Be the hero of your own story. You already have a good idea of who you want to be, so everything else is secondary. "No matter what other people think or say, you should always go your own way."

Try not to think too deeply. Consider what is happening right now. You shouldn't be concerned about the past or the future. Consider what you can do right now to make things easier for yourself tomorrow. Make some moves toward the expansion. You should consider carefully, but when it's time to act, you should put your thoughts aside and get to work. Bring some peace and quietness to your mind. Avoid going in a direction that's going to make you feel bad. It is a pit of despair for you, and you will make things worse for yourself if you continue down this path. Therefore, listen to your gut. Put an end to those pointless thoughts running through your head, and don't let the problems of the past weigh you down now. Your mind and emotions will become cluttered with unimportant thoughts as a result. Put some effort into overcoming each of your negative thoughts one at a time. and follow both what your head tells you and what your heart tells you to do. I can assure you that the answer is within your heart. It is worth remembering that although you can't see the full staircase from the bottom of the stairwell, you should never let that stop you from making the first step up the stairs.

Keep your next move a secret from everyone else. It's not necessary to share everything with everyone. You should keep certain things to yourself. Work in relative obscurity if you want to accomplish something truly remarkable. Take quiet, methodical steps. Put in the effort to achieve your objectives without notifying others. When you tell other people about your hopes and ambitions, the likelihood of achieving those goals decreases since those other people are more likely to criticize you and try to convince you to change your mind. Now is the time to keep your ambitions a secret from others until you have achieved them. If no one knows what you are doing, then no one will try to stop you from doing it. The less information about yourself that you give out to other people, the more control you will have over them and the greater success you will have overall. Therefore, maintain your privacy if you want to climb the ladder of success all the way to the top. Keep your plans super-secret, folks, and let your result make noise.

Never stop educating yourself. Learning is an ongoing process throughout life. It's not like you just take some tests, get your diploma, and then everything is over with. Learning is something that continues throughout your entire life. You acquire new knowledge with each new step. Therefore, continue your education forever. Learn everything that piques your interest.

You have the opportunity to acquire new knowledge on a daily basis. Therefore, seize every possible educational opportunity. Learn something completely new. Show that you can do it. Create objectives for the day and make sure you meet them. Educate yourself on everything from the smallest details to the most significant ones. Therefore, make the most of every experience in your life. It may also be:

> "I'm going to work a different route this morning."
>
> Starting out in the process of learning a new language.
>
> Trying out different foods

- DIY projects for interior home decoration
- Beginning of the reading
- Gaining knowledge about fundamental house maintenance.
- Rearranging the items in your cupboard in a different fashion.
- Learning how to write computer code.

Always look to improve your knowledge and skills. Gain knowledge and insight through your academic pursuits. Develop yourself, try new things, keep your mind active, and strive to reach new heights. Just go at your own pace, but make sure you never stop moving forward. The wonderful thing about education is that it is something that can never be taken away from you.

Surround yourself with people who are motivational and uplifting. It is of the utmost significance to populate your immediate environment with brilliant individuals who possess a vision and are making significant efforts to demonstrate that vision. They will encourage you to go closer to achieving your goals. Look around you and on social media sites for other people who work in your line of work who you may connect with. Get in touch with people who have been successful in your fields and start networking with them. Communicate with them. Engage in conversation with them. Observe the manner in which they perform each task. Gain wisdom from their experience. Consider the input that is positive. Put yourself in situations where you can learn and develop alongside other people. You're a product of your environment. Therefore, if you want to become the best, you need to surround yourself with the best.

Your circle is crucial. Make an informed decision. Be positive. Put your faith in yourself if you want to live a life filled with joy and achievement.

"Surround yourself with people who will only make you stronger," the saying goes.

A hope that is allowed to fade away without being pursued will one day become a nightmare.

– Allan Mandindi

CHAPTER 7

Discover your Personality

The power of the general populace to bring about change is hindered by the widespread absence of positive thinking. You will never be able to convince anyone of anything unless you can bring your thoughts and your own reality into harmony with one another. Accepting oneself is the first step toward loving oneself. The fact that your habits and personality qualities are not typical does not make them any less valuable than they would be otherwise. The spectrum of colours that make up a rainbow is what gives it its aesthetic value. If we were just able to choose between black and white, our lives would be considerably less complicated.

My time in Lilongwe allowed me to take stock of my life, figure out who I am, and comprehend the purpose behind my existence. I had no choice but to confront the reality of the situation and acknowledge the steps that needed to be taken if I wanted to succeed. From my vantage point, I could see how my background and the things I had experienced might potentially impact my development. When I eventually accepted myself for who I am, I was able to turn my struggles into a platform from which I could launch myself toward achievement.

Realizing how you are different from the people around you, beginning with your own family and the community that is immediately surrounding you, is the first step in accepting your individuality and embracing your uniqueness. When you are at ease with who you are as an individual, you are in a better position to put your uniqueness to good use and contribute to making the world a better place. Being original is going to be challenging for you if you can't figure out what makes you unique. Have faith in yourself and your abilities. If you don't believe in yourself, no one else will support what you're trying to do.

Put your energy into something that matters: When you are aware of the goals you wish to achieve, it is a waste of time to attempt to accomplish those goals using the strategy of another person. The level of dedication you put into accomplishing your goals will determine how far you get in life. Consider what happens to a person whose beliefs are agnostic: they are susceptible to being convinced of anything. Never accept a life that lacks excitement and adventure. Put yourself in uncomfortable situations by doing things that will leave others with a strong impression. I went through my formative years alongside a large number of classmates at my high school but unfortunately, only a small fraction of those friends are still living at this point in time. You won't be able to make an impact unless you constantly keep a watchful eye on the bigger picture. It's unfortunate that many of us lack this quality due to the many distractions in our modern society, and it's even more difficult to acquire if you were raised in a group of people who were similarly myopic.

You are well aware of all that must be done in order for you to succeed in completing your mission. When you articulate your objectives, you provide replies to queries with highly personal importance. Who do you want to be, what do you want to achieve, and how do you plan to get to where you want to be? You will be able to shape your long-term life goals and become an individual when you achieve them if you answer these questions in an honest manner.

Learn to improve yourself by becoming aware of your shortcomings. Everyone has their own individual set of positives and negatives to offer. Your shortcomings have the potential to be either strengths or limits, depending on how you choose to handle them. When confronted with the possibility of placing oneself in harm's way, a person's lack of strength manifests itself as a sort of cowardice. When your weaknesses are more prominent than your talents, it is difficult to make headway in your life. When I ran into my first significant roadblock, I didn't just throw in the towel and stop working toward my objectives. I needed to give myself a challenge by accomplishing something spectacular, and that required me to take some risks. In my situation, it was joining the army of the United Kingdom. It could be anything as simple as beginning a new business or as involved as preparing for an important exam in your mind. The single most important factor in your overall level of success will be your mindset and how you choose to overcome challenges. The worry about how other people would respond to one's decisions has inhibited many people from doing great things in their lives. The purpose of offering criticism in a constructive manner is to encourage growth rather than lower self-esteem. You cannot expect life to be easy, and as a result, you must be ready to deal with challenges and difficulties that will put your skills to the test. It will be easier for you to manage the stress that comes with standing out if you are aware of your shortcomings and actively seek to fix them.

Raise your companion with the pertinent mindset: You are a reflection of the individuals in your immediate environment. Because of this knowledge gap, smaller minds are unable to communicate effectively with larger ones. If you surround yourself with people who are average or below, you will never get above that level, no matter how intelligent you are. People who fall under the category of "normal" don't create, develop answers, or take risks. They are a perfect example of what the average person would be like. Because of this, many people are unable to rise above their current social standing. The influence of one's contemporaries was a significant downside to life in Kamzimbi, despite the fact that there were many positive qualities to this way of life. A person whose mind is already vulnerable can be profoundly affected by the negative habits of others, particularly those with whom one engages in social interactions. This is especially true of the people with whom one associates socially. Because of their poor choices, the company that they kept was a major contributor to the unfortunate consequences that occurred for so many other people. If you want to distinguish yourself from the crowd, you should surround yourself with people who share your worldview. Through interaction with other people and the sharing of your experiences, you can learn and develop as a person. Individuals who are successful often have access to opportunities, thanks to the people they know and trust. It's possible that this is the reason you aren't meeting the right individuals in your life.

Develop the Substance of Hard Work: If you can't master even the most basic skills, you won't be able to move on to higher levels. No matter how young and unskilled you feel, the things that you do, even on a small scale, matter a great deal. It is important to keep in mind that working for long periods of time does not automatically correspond to being diligent. When we talk about diligence, what we really mean is the capacity to generate results in a way that is both reliable and effective. A strong work ethic and consistent working habits are both components of the personality trait of dedication. Someone who is diligent is capable of effectively managing their time, establishing and achieving goals, toiling genuinely, and resisting the urge to give up easily. People, in general, don't put in a lot of effort and when they do, they're usually satisfied with relatively moderate levels of achievement.

During the time that I spent trying to join the British Army, I was not the only person who was admitted to the service, nor was I the only person who was deployed to Afghanistan, but I persevered and this resulted in my receiving Her Majesty's Queen Medal of Service, an award in recognition of my efforts. Those who are diligent always provide their absolute best effort, regardless of how little the work at hand may be. They stand apart from everything else that is available, which ultimately contributes to their long-term success.

CHAPTER 8

Build a Vision to Set Yourself Apart

Even though there are around 30 billion other stars in the universe right now, the sun is the one that sticks out the most because it has the most brilliant light. The names of today's great people are often associated with the sun because of how they stand out from their contemporaries.

If you differentiate yourself from the other people in the room, you increase the likelihood that someone will notice you because you are standing out from the crowd. It is not enough to be one of a kind; instead, you should challenge yourself to exceed because, when you do so regularly, you establish yourself as a role model for others to follow.

"What makes you unique could at times feel like a burden, but it is not meant to be." And the majority of the time, it is what makes you incredible. Actress Emma Stone appears in the picture here.

A brilliant intellect must be willing to accept the fact that it must behave unpredictably. Being noticeably different from the majority of people is not a negative trait to possess. The people around you might find you peculiar, but because of your skills and originality, you'll remain in their minds for a very long time.

I realized that if I did not construct a vision for myself while I was in school in a distant village where there was little incentive and exposure to new things, I would not accomplish very much. If I lived there, I would make my dreams come true just like the other people who have done so. I will be the first to say that it was challenging at first, but I was determined to reach my objective.

This chapter will talk about why you should stand out and how you can do so.

What does it mean, exactly, to have one's own identity?

The Merriam-Webster Dictionary describes the trait termed "distinctively" as being one that is both exceptional and appealing. On the other hand, "different" refers to something that is not ordinary or common. According to the definitions of both of these words, the phrase "uncommon" can be utilized to describe an individual who is noticeably dissimilar from the norm.

When other people have a favourable image of you, they will tell their friends and family about the things you do that impress them. It is impossible to conceal a bright light in the dark since it sheds light on the area immediately around it. As an original and distinct individual, you are gradually bringing about constructive change.

To have a greatness mindset, you must be unique. You need to live your life differently, behave differently, work differently, and communicate differently, and you need to be willing to make a difference in the world around you. Indeed, obeying the rules won't affect you, but the tiny things you do that other people take for granted can make a significant difference.

My development was aided by the challenges that I faced in Lilongwe. It's possible that you won't truly value something until you've earned it through toil and sweat. The process of changing into a different person is filled with challenges that can either help you define your destiny or derail it entirely.

Why should anyone pay attention to you?

Since our fates are so dissimilar, no two people ever take the same route through life. People who spend their whole lives trying to be like other people will never achieve greatness, and the rest of the world will view them as nothing more than a carbon copies. When you grow up in a rural location as I did, it makes things much more challenging. If you don't have the appropriate people to steer you in the correct direction, you run the risk of settling into a comfortable life of ignorance and mediocrity.

Why do so many people act like sheep and follow the herd? People have a natural aversion to alteration since they are used to things continuing in the same manner as before. Even if that is not the case, action will be regarded as appropriate if it is taken at a time when the world as a whole is moving in the right direction. A person who is visibly distinct and who finds novel ways to move could be considered weird by others.

People will judge you negatively if you have a unique appearance. Even members of your own family and circle of friends will have negative things to say about your decisions and behaviours. I do not doubt that my dad was a good example for me to follow in life, but I know not everyone has that opportunity.

It is difficult to attain greatness without facing challenges and receiving constructive criticism. As you go, you are guaranteed to encounter challenges and roadblocks at some point. Society will tell you, "This is the way you do things, so pay attention. If you don't do things this way, you won't succeed." To overcome this obstacle, all you need to do is close your eyes and act in a manner consistent with who you are.

The following are a few reasons you should differentiate yourself from the rest of the crowd:

It helps you work toward the accomplishment of your objective: There is a purpose for the existence of humans. We are endowed with the skills, talents, creative potential, and intellectual capacity to have an effect, either directly or indirectly, on the lives of those who are in our immediate environment. If you do not have a clear idea of what it is that you want to accomplish, you will never be able to get there. Individuals who possess similar skills and talents strive, just like everyone else, to set themselves apart. The panel of judges at a singing competition thinks you have what it takes to be a vocalist. However, in order to make it through to the final round of the competition and have their voices judged as the best, contestants need to put in a lot of effort to improve their singing. To achieve greatness, talent alone will never be sufficient; one must also put in a lot of hard work on themselves. Despite the fact that I was exceptionally talented and intelligent, I was not accepted into the University of Malawi. In addition, the opportunity to pursue higher education in another country is not open to everyone. My family members might have chastised me for quitting my accounting studies, but I realized this was not for me. I believed I was meant for greater things, and I have no regrets about my decision. I kept working on myself, and when the opportunity arose, I took it. Improving your talents on a daily basis will take you out of the crowded space of normal individuals. This is why you must stand out. People who follow the crowd lose themselves in the process because they have no goal to accomplish. Having a purpose allows you to pick the best path and make the best decisions. Because you know where you're going, the proper decisions you make will eventually differ from those of others around you.

It aids in influencing your surroundings. The environment plays a key role in your growth. When you are born, your immediate family becomes the first socializing agent. They teach you what is good and bad, as well as your society's norms and obligations. You are also exposed to other institutions such as school, religious organizations, and even peer groups. The internet, because of technological advancement, also serves as a socialization agent. People must follow a course in society, which may be difficult for creative brains who continuously think outside the box. Furthermore, a child like me, who comes from a low-income family, may find it difficult to challenge the ideals and expectations of that setting due to a lack of physical and mental exposure. I was certain that I would be a light of hope, and I refused to accept anything less. I never waited for others to openly support me because I knew what I needed to do. When a youngster breaks down the limits imposed by his or her background by being distinct from other members of that society, it has a beneficial impact on the socialization environment and gives hope to other people who want to be successful.

It increases your self-assurance. Another reason you should stand out is to boost your self-esteem. You are not afraid to fail when you are confident. Failure is frowned upon in society, making it difficult for people to take risks. Many individuals are where they are today because they are terrified of failure, but those who rise beyond failure will find greatness. The confidence you gain will motivate you to work harder until you attain your objectives. A person who is self-assured has high self-esteem. It takes a lot of guts to go against the majority's ideas, and when you consistently go against the grain, your self-esteem rises because people respect you for who you are and what you have accomplished. Push yourself harder and train your mind to be resilient even when you fail. When I didn't get into the University of Malawi, no one could blame me for settling for less, but I never gave up. It inspired me to try harder because my story would not be the same in perpetuity. Because my thinking was different, this increased my confidence.

It allows you to develop. Growth is a necessary component of human development. When you stand out, you improve faster by learning from your failures and taking on bigger tasks. Every day, a high achiever seeks to learn new things. A mind that is not teachable will never achieve greatness. Did you notice how long it took me to achieve my goals? Many people strive to achieve greatness in a short period of time. Their thinking is not patient enough to go through the process of self-development. If I had taken the easy route, my achievement would have been early and fleeting. You must understand that excellent leaders engage with one another in order to progress, which is why their circle is so limited. The audience is content with mediocrity, and the vast majority does not even read. Changing demands a lot of sacrifices, and developing is an important part of that. Do not rely solely on your wits. Learn something new today.

It allows you to be genuine. The world will see someone who is noticeably different from an authentic person. Because many people lack the imagination and discipline to improve themselves, authenticity is in short supply. It is simpler to blend into a crowd with no purpose than to stand out. However, if you have a strong desire to achieve, you must strive for honesty. It will not be an easy journey to the point of achievement because gold requires a lot of heat to become pure.

To keep an open mind. Someone who is open-minded believes in the unimaginable. People must have laughed at the Wright brothers back then. They built an airplane prototype. Many others thought the discovery of electric energy was ridiculous. Nonetheless, outstanding inventors and their contributions to humanity are remembered.

People with an open mind are problem solvers. They do not, unlike the rest of the throng, fold their arms in response to the challenges that surround them. They deal with the situation directly and without giving up since they are fundamentally different. When you have an open mind, you are not afraid to ask questions or receive criticism. A closed mind will always be blind to new perspectives on ideas, whereas a free mind will never be terrified of change.

Sometimes in life, we need to find that particular something within ourselves that will set us apart and distinguish us from the rest of society. This is not a simple process for many people, but it is worth the effort. During my childhood growing up in Malawi, I had no idea that there was something about me that set me apart. I kept exploring while trying hard not to do what everyone else was doing. While in secondary school, I realized I had something that others didn't, and I began to cultivate it. My strong ambition and commitment to succeed led me to discover a passion for sports at a young age, and weightlifting was where I found solace. My athletic talent and resilience served as stepping stones on my path to greatness. I learned to believe in myself after winning the Mr. Phwezi Powerlift Competition. I knew I had a special talent that I needed to keep. I arrived in England in 2003 intending to study accounting. I spent two years trying to fit into an atmosphere where I couldn't. One could argue that it was a waste of time, but this was my opportunity to reset, reconsider, or reorganize. I was frustrated since I wasn't making the desired progress.

I opted to join the British Army in 2008. My time in the army was the best of my life. I kept doing what I loved, weightlifting, and reconnected with my talents. This made me feel better about myself. I was good at what I did. In 2010, I was sent to the 6th Supply Regiment in Gutersloh, Germany. We were all encouraged to participate in sports in the army because it was part of the culture. When I arrived at my unit, many young and active guys had taken up jogging. I had to consider what sport I could participate in. This is where I considered doing anything that would make me appear different. I discovered that powerlifting existed in the army, but no one in my regiment participated in it. I immediately signed up for the power lift. I was invited to my first competition, which I promptly won in my category, and I was even highlighted in a newsletter distributed to all British Army soldiers in Germany. My name was renowned throughout Army Headquarters. My friends began to question how I had risen to the senior level in such a short period. Some of them were excellent athletes, but they were competing in an already crowded arena. This is the dilemma that many young people face today: failing to recognize their natural skills and instead, following what others are doing in business, career, and other areas of life. We need to find something unique about ourselves or our businesses that will set us apart from the crowd. This should always be our primary technique for cultivating a tremendous attitude. I was able to be successful in my army career by following this path, even though I opted to quit when I was recommended for advancement to pursue my goal after being awarded a scholarship to study politics. My current occupation is not that of a powerlifter. However, as a result of that experience, I was able to discover my strengths and break through certain hurdles in my personal development, which has led me on a wonderful path. What I discovered was that I could pursue a career that I was passionate about—I'd wanted to make a difference in people's lives since I was in elementary school.

You must learn to be unique and devise a strategy that will set you apart from the crowd. Utilize your God-given natural abilities, since these are what will make you unique. Continue to learn, and don't be afraid to make mistakes. Those who are experts at what they do build their reputation by learning from their errors. If your natural gift is your voice, learn to use it to your advantage. Nowadays, thanks to social media, one does not need to go through an audition to become a superstar or popular. There are numerous avenues through which young people can achieve success.

We live in a highly competitive society where being recognized requires great ability and subtlety. One thing to remember is that we all have a specific gift within us that has to be discovered. You can't claim a strength you're not aware of.

CHAPTER 9

The Suggestive Influence of your Mind

I give thanks to God that I have been able to make significant progress toward realizing the goals I have set for myself. Everything that I had envisioned up to this point has become a reality.

First, the goal was to earn a master's degree and fulfil a lifelong ambition. At first, I thought this was a dream, but I worked up the guts to go for my goals even though the odds were stacked against me, and I was successful. As long as you remember what it is you want out of life and don't let your aspirations cloud your judgment, it is not a bad thing to have lofty objectives or aspirations. You might get ridiculed by other people, but you have to push through it and keep your attention fixed squarely on the objective at hand while still moving on with the activities that excite you the most.

Have you ever come across the concept known as the "Law of Attraction"? The belief that our experiences are produced by our thoughts and feelings and that whatever it is that we focus our attention on will be brought into our lives is referred to as the "Law of Attraction."

To put it another way, we are exactly what it is that we want and desire. The longer you engage in a particular activity, the closer you will become to that activity. For example, if you want to become a billionaire, you should start by seeing how other millionaires carry out their daily activities, deal with the challenges of life, and interact with other people. You won't have to wait long before others start attaching to you as a unit, and you'll also start getting closer to achieving your goals.

To emphasize this point, everything that I have pictured coming to fruition has happened. People of high standing whom I had only ever imagined interacting with have suddenly acknowledged me as a member of their community. Never have any doubts about yourself; instead, set goals for yourself and, above all else, have faith in who you are. Even the Bible mentions faith in Hebrews chapter 11 verse 1: "Now faith is the substance of things hoped for, the proof of things not seen."

When we have faith in ourselves and believe in ourselves, we are able to accomplish great things that we never would have thought we were capable of doing.

In life, you should never give up and you should never try to focus on the negative; instead, you should concentrate on growth. Strive to be a more admirable person today than you were yesterday.

People say that "giving yourself to continuous learning, practical experiences, and knowledge has the power to change lives," which was first said by Allan Mandindi.

SHOOT AT THE SKY ABOVE

Why Is It Important to Aim High When Dreaming?

This is something that we constantly hear. It is tacked up on the wall of every single restroom in every primary school. When you are unsure of the path your life will take, your mother will tell you this. Dream big. In concept, having huge dreams is a wonderful thing to do, but in practice, it's far simpler to say than to do. Having said that, if we do not have ambitious goals, we will never realize our full potential. If we want to accomplish what we set out to do in life, we have to have ambitious goals. That is, in a nutshell, what it means to "dream big." However, we are going to go deeper by discussing these five reasons it is so vital:

Optimism is the key to building momentum. The mind is everything, which has been paraphrased numerous times by motivational speakers. What do you believe you will become? When we allow ourselves to dream big, our brains are activated, and we begin to become aware of opportunities and possibilities that were previously hidden from us. As we continue to realize that others believe in our great aspirations, the positivity that we exhibit will bring even more connections and opportunities into our reality. Our unwavering faith in the reality of our goals generates forward momentum that grows exponentially.

You Redirect Your Attention: As was indicated before, when you put your attention on the strategies and activities that will bring you closer to realizing your goals, you start to become aware of new approaches to achieving certain goals. When you put your attention on discovering solutions, you will find those solutions. Those who, however, concentrate an excessive amount of their attention on the things that may go wrong on their path to achievement are more inclined to quit when confronted with obstacles.

They won't be able to continue fighting forever. What we put our attention on, expands. When you are committed to turning your dream into reality, you tend to concentrate on the successes and the lessons that you have learned along the way, which in turn gives you more of the same kinds of blessings.

The Capacity to Bounce Back After Struggle: No matter how meticulously we plan or how assiduously we work, we will inevitably fail. It's not something we look forward to, but when we fail while having huge dreams and shooting for the stars, we're actually failing forward. It will hurt for a moment, but when you get back up, you will feel ten times stronger and more resilient, and you will have more information than you did before. We start to understand that the only way to truly fail is to make no effort at all.

Time Management Becomes Important: When you hear the word "dreamer," it's possible that the first thing that comes to mind isn't exceptional time management skills. However, people who are truly committed to turning their ideal life into a reality always make sure to make the most of the time they have. They know that time is the most valuable thing they have, and they know that if they want to reach their goals, they have to make good use of this asset.

The Development of Confidence: You might have believed that completing this quest was impossible before you really started it. You used to regularly adopt phrases like "can't" and "impossible" in your vocabulary, but once you start reaching for the stars and seeing the results, your confidence will skyrocket in all facets of your life!

CHAPTER 10

Boost your Morale and Confidence

Believe in yourself, develop the right mindset, surround yourself with people who think like you, practice self-discipline, remain consistent, have a strong drive to learn, don't be afraid to try something new, and keep going until you succeed. These are some of the things that will help you achieve success.

I'll begin with the first one and work my way through the rest, explaining each step in greater detail as I go.

PUT YOUR TRUST IN YOUR OWN ABILITIES

One must trust in one's capabilities in order to have self-confidence. It's having faith that what you want to accomplish can be done and is within your grasp. If you have faith in yourself, you will be able to overcome your self-doubt and take the actions that are necessary to attain the goals that you have set for yourself. Despite appearances, one of the most challenging parts of being a young person in today's society is fitting in. This gives rise to issues such as "How am I supposed to believe in myself when I am not even certain that I am on the correct track?" Yea! Fear is the primary motivating factor in this situation. When other people found out that I hadn't lived up to their expectations of me, I was terrified of what they would say about me. The days after I found out I wouldn't be attending the University of Malawi were excruciating, but I never wavered in my commitment to achieving greatness, and the idea of giving up on my goals never crossed my mind. I decided to enlist in the military while I waited, and after achieving success there, I decided to stay in the service for another five years as I continued my pursuit of higher education. Later on, I came across a flyer advertising a political science degree at Manchester Metropolitan University. Although I did not meet the prerequisites, I made the decision not to take the chance of not being accepted into the program. However, I had only completed the General Certificate of Education, and they were seeking someone with an A-level. Despite this, I went ahead and submitted my application since I was confident in my ability to be accepted. After the interview, I was strongly encouraged to create an essay which I did, and as a result, I am currently enrolled as a Master's student at Manchester Metropolitan University. What if I lacked the appropriate credentials which would make me feel less confident in my abilities? The key to living is not to sit around and do nothing. The fact that I've gotten this far in life is a direct result of the ambitious nature I've always had.

Everyone on the planet must consider this. If you struggle to believe in yourself, no one else should expect you to convince anyone else to do so. Nobody has the time to go after phantoms, but if you exude confidence in who you are and what you do, other people will have no option but to take your word for it. You are the first individual to see the full potential of the seeds that have been planted deep within you for your achievement, and they have been there all along. Only the results you produce can serve as actual evidence.

Taking calculated risks in any pursuit, whether it be academic, personal, or professional, requires a healthy dose of self-assurance. You need to have confidence in yourself, your abilities, and the things that attract you to take the plunge into business or any other activity. The foundation of strong leadership is self-belief because it paves the way for the leader to confidently guide and motivate their followers. Having faith in oneself is the bedrock of great leadership.

You are your very first audience, and you have the most support from me. You need to be able to work and make modifications even when others are not constantly monitoring what you are doing.

There are only so many of you in the world. Make something, regardless of how insignificant it might appear at the time; learn as much as you can, both formally and informally, about yourself, and you'll see that it was worth it. The payoff is worth it for those who persevere and put in the effort. Simply continue in the same direction you've been heading.

When framed in this manner, the question, "Why is it so important to have faith in yourself?" becomes easier to answer. It's not complicated: having faith in yourself is necessary if you want to bring about the improvements you see in your life.

To have genuine faith in oneself, one needs to look at things from every possible angle. You have to have mental and emotional control over yourself if you want to achieve at your highest level. Developing self-assurance and falling in love with the aspects of your personality and the experiences of your life that make you, well, you are also components of this process.

HARNESSING AN ADEQUATE MINDSET

It is essential to cultivate the appropriate mindset in order to achieve success since the Oxford English Dictionary defines Mindset as "decision theory" and "general systems theory." One way to define a person's or a group's mindset is as an underlying collection of beliefs, values, and methods of thinking held by that person or group. The worldview or philosophy of life of a person is another factor that might be examined while analyzing the origin of their attitude. Carol Dweck, a researcher and psychologist, has distinguished between two distinct mindsets, which she calls the "fixed mindset" and the "growth mindset." To be more specific, what does it mean to have a "stuck mindset," though? People of any age who believe that their intelligence, talents, and personality attributes are immutable and hence fixed are said to have a "fixed mentality." The phrase "fixed mindset" was coined by psychologist Carol Dweck. They believe that everyone is born with the same amount of intelligence and that we are unable to further improve our talents as we grow older. Because it causes people to be unwilling to try new things, this way of thinking is frequently referred to as the "restricted mindset." If you're unable to break out of your fixed mindset, you won't be able to progress as a person or have any other kind of reality. When I get the chance to talk to young people, one of the things that I make sure to convey to them is that they should "focus on their thinking." When a person finally caves into the limitations imposed by their mind, their entire existence begins to spiral downward in a negative direction. You are the only person who can set boundaries for your potential, and if you approach your work with the right frame of mind, you have the ability to accomplish anything you set your mind to. The only limit to your potential is the one you place on yourself, having faith in one's capabilities rather than depending on the expertise of others.

According to Carol Dweck, who is the inventor of the theory of fixed mindsets, having such a perspective prevents you from accomplishing impossible things. Because they are concerned about what other people will think of them or the choices they make, many people are reluctant to try new things, make decisions, or even just speak their thoughts. It is not necessary to have a wide-ranging and unbounded vision. Always remember to maintain a good mental attitude. The other primary way of looking at things is known as the "growth attitude." An "I can do it" attitude toward learning and development is an example of what we mean when we talk about having a growth mindset. We are all aware that one of the most important factors in leading a happy and successful life is cultivating a positive mental attitude. However, how exactly can we make our own lives and the lives of our children better through the application of this amazing resource? A "growth mentality" is the term used to describe an optimistic frame of mind. When viewed from such a perspective, anything is feasible. In contrast to the old mentality, the new one, known as the growth mentality, accepts and stimulates the development of creative thinking as well as fresh techniques. Those who believe in this outlook, as opposed to those who believe in the static, embrace expansion. Each young person has his/her method that he/she uses to evaluate his/her abilities and potential. Those who are mentally mired in a rut are certain that they will never be in a position to put forward novel concepts for evaluation, regardless of how realistic those concepts may appear to be. They steer clear of circumstances in which they are exposed to the possibility of making a mistake or of experiencing the sensation of being overextended.

Those that have a growth mentality, on the other hand, view failures and difficulties for what they are: opportunities to develop and expand their knowledge. To acquire this mentality, all you need to do is to convince yourself that you are capable of achieving your goals.

You should encourage your child to write in a journal about how they overcome difficult circumstances. Choose some books to read and movies to watch that will inspire you to keep going. Always be sure to acknowledge and praise your child's efforts whenever they achieve something. In contrast to the pessimistic and reactive outlook of the fixed mindset which is characterized by the phrase "I can't," the growth mindset takes an "I can" (freedom) approach to life. It isn't always easy to have a growth mentality because circumstances can turn out differently than expected, but the idea that you can become exceptional if you're consistent can keep you moving in the right direction.

As I've indicated in the past, there have been instances in which I lacked self-assurance; nonetheless, I was able to persevere through these periods because I knew that one day I would be able to make a positive impact on the lives of others. I've always been the kind of person who wants to lend a hand to people who are struggling, one who reaches out to others and offers my assistance in the hope of easing their pain. This is the truth in my opinion, and it became the impetus behind all I did.

The great Indian leader Mahatma Gandhi famously remarked, "You must become the change that you wish to see in the world." This was one of my favourite quotes for a good portion of my life since it served as a constant reminder that I not only had the ability to improve my own life but also the lives of those I cared about and the world at large.

BUILD A POSITIVE REFERENCE GROUP

Hang out with folks that have the same morals and perspective on life as you do. The people you spend the most time with can have a huge influence on how you think of yourself as well as how you spend your time. They have the ability to change a person's view of themselves and how they see the world. Therefore, maintaining positive relationships with others is essential. Those of your friends and coworkers who are genuinely invested in your achievement will be the ones who both motivate you and push you to expand your horizons. They inspire you to believe in your own capabilities and work toward improving yourself. After spending time with them, you will invariably look at the world through a more optimistic lens. On the other hand, it's possible that you have friends or acquaintances who have a persistently pessimistic and resentful attitude. Even if you make a conscious effort to avoid them, you may still be affected by the outcomes of the poor choices they make. The expression "Show me your friend, and I'll tell who you are" refers to the idea that the people with whom you surround yourself reveal a great deal about your personality and character.

Psychologists believe that your perspective on the world can be significantly shaped by the circle of friends and acquaintances with whom you maintain regular touch. If you and another person are not going in the same direction, it is considered courteous not to waste time by going in the direction that the other person is going. Your goals could be stifled if you choose to work for the wrong firm.

You are well aware of the many different factors that can contribute to the diversity of a student body. Some of these factors include home schooling, cultural origins, and others.

I can recall there being both positive and negative effects at the local school I attended back then; many young men got involved in several crimes despite the fact that they were entirely misled by their classmates. My time in

Kamzimbi instilled in me the importance of meaningful relationships and the worth of exercising my own free will. Many young people give in to their fantasies because they lack the moral fortitude to make choices that are in their best interests. My experiences reflecting on my past have taught me how important it is to establish and uphold strong personal standards. I could have easily been one of those troubled youths you see on the streets today if it weren't for the associations I've cultivated that have helped me demonstrate my authority. I am grateful to the individuals who have made positive contributions to my reputation.

Whatever you put into life is exactly what you will get back. Great people are able to plan for the future even when they have no resources available to them to work with. You should avoid spending time with people who do not motivate you to enhance your employability for the future. If conversing with other people will not move your life or your goals forward, you should avoid doing so.

It is in your best interest to part ways with that person and look for someone else who is heading in the same general direction as you.

Discipline is "the correction or control of oneself for the goal of improvement." "Self-government," for example, can be defined as "a group of people who control and make decisions for a country, state, or other entity." This definition makes the most effective use of language given the circumstances, and as a result, I advocate using it. Now, the definition that was presented earlier is a personal one, which means "you are the one who has the authority to control and make decisions for yourself." This suggests that practicing self-discipline is a choice, as is accepting responsibility for one's actions and realizing one's ambitions; these are all decisions that can only be made by the individual concerned.

It has been demonstrated that exercising self-control is an effective method of motivating oneself to occupy the ethical high ground. This helps one arrive at a moral conclusion self-control is an effective method of motivating oneself to occupy the ethical high ground. This helps one arrive at moral conclusions. People who adhere to the self-discipline school of thought feel that doing so strengthens a person's sense of responsibility for the manner in which they conduct themselves.

In order to sustain a culture of ethics in the workplace, intensive self-discipline training is necessary. It is not difficult to conform to moral standards if one is already determined to abandon unethical practices. This sort of self-discipline might be helpful in the fight against unethical and unlawful means of getting things done. The person is able to withstand the moral pressure of their peers and will not give in to temptation. The individual is able to withstand the moral pressure of their peers.

Discipline has been the main idea in my life, and it has helped me become the responsible and polite person I am today.

These qualities are lacking in the lives of today's youths because they are only concerned with fitting into the crowd and are not concerned with doing what is right. Even if it might look like there is no hope in the world right now, you have the power to alter that.

Consistency: In my experience, putting a lot of effort into anything constantly yields a substantial return in the long run.

According to Merriam-Webster's definition, for anything to be consistent, it must retain the same qualities across the course of time and in a variety of settings. People I've seen just couldn't keep up, and eventually, they realized that they were just spinning their wheels and accomplishing nothing. I've seen this happen. If something is important enough to complete, then it is also important enough to do very well at. It doesn't matter what you decide to do, because everything will turn out OK. Stick with what you love doing, even if it isn't profitable just now, rather than wandering from one location to another in quest of something that doesn't exist.

In today's society, many young people don't want to do hands-on work that could change the world because they quickly lose hope and give up when they don't see results right away. Your work will grow more beautiful and valuable as you become more consistent, and you should always keep in mind that nothing of value is ever straightforward or easy. Indeed, things aren't always rosy at the beginning, but they say that time is a revelation only to those who are consistent in what they do. Don't let anyone trick you into rushing through life; most of the time, things aren't all roses at the beginning.

Please make me smart. Read! I look forward to the day that I am famous. What can you do to help further the cause of the greater good? To achieve greatness, one must be willing to put in a lot of effort and have a lot of patience. Young people who want to be successful in their ways in life need to cultivate a culture of consistency in their daily lives. Your future will be directly influenced by the choices you make right now. Have you identified the activities in which you excel the most? Do not give up; the benefits will quickly outweigh the work that you put in.

The urge to gain additional knowledge is one thing that, on account of pride and ego, is frequently disregarded. Because they mistakenly believe it would help them learn more, a lot of people spend less time listening and more time talking. It is essential to have the ability to listen more than you can speak if you wish to achieve the highest levels of success. We live in a world that is always evolving, and new hints are unearthed daily. Because of this, it is now possible to share information with anyone, at any time, regardless of age, socioeconomic status, or anything else of the sort.

Truth and comprehension are not subject to the sole possession of any one individual. Gaining wisdom involves a commitment to lifelong study and attentiveness. There is always something new to pick up from other people, regardless of how knowledgeable you assume you already are. You have not yet uncovered the vast majority of the knowledge that is currently available. Keep in mind that it is just as important to receive information as it is to provide it. A sage from long ago made the observation that "excellent teachers are also superb listeners." I became a better listener when I realized that every person I have a conversation with has a distinct point of view that is based on their area of expertise. Since it is impossible to be an expert in every topic, the more you listen, the more you learn, and the more you study, the more others will believe what you say.

It is not necessary to be afraid to experiment with new things because, the majority of the time, we just learn by imitating others. Some people are scared to try out new strategies for the simple fact that they are terrified of failing.

If you want to differentiate yourself from the rest of the pack, you have to be authentic to who you are and fight the temptation to behave in a way that is consistent with accepted norms by employing a creative mentality. Being unique is what separates you from everyone else. There is a saturation of the market due to the production of products that are identical to one another; an abundance of competitors in every arena of life, from the home to the school and beyond.

A flawed perspective on the world might produce a mental block in the form of anxiety that no one will be interested in what you make. It sounds like you are very certain that your product won't be successful in the marketplace. Be confident in your abilities, yet maintain an open mind to the possibility that they could use some work while ignoring the opinions of others.

Do not be afraid to deviate from the norm and become the person you were always destined to be.

The reality is that you should be more concerned about how well you blend in with the crowd than you should be about how well you stick out. Don't attempt to be anyone else; just be yourself and own your qualities.

When one person finds a gap in the market and fills it in a way that no one else has done before, that is the beginning of an invention. Our lives aren't meant to have results that are the same as each other. Instead, they are meant to have results that are different from and add to each other.

Excellent thinkers are also excellent doers, and excellent warriors are excellent thinkers. Being inhibited by fear prevents one from reaching their full potential. You have to be willing to take the risk of really putting your ideas into practice if you want to become the next great inventor.

What, in your opinion, enabled men such as Aristotle and Karl Marx to become pioneering figures in the domains in which they worked? Because they had original thoughts, you too, have the potential to pioneer new territory.

What do you think the key is to the success of exceptional people, whether they are men or women? Could it be that difficult to say? Some people did what everyone else was too chicken to do. Young people should not automatically believe that simply trying anything new is all that is required of them, as this is the sincere advice I have for them.

You should never throw in the towel. I strongly recommend that you do not give up and that you never give up. No matter how difficult things become, you should never even entertain the thought of giving up. There are both good times and difficult times. Even if it's not always easy, it's necessary to get through the challenges of life and figure out what you need to know in order to move forward. I remember when I was in school, and I had every excuse to give up on my dreams, such as living in a thatched house with mice crawling through my legs every night, not meeting up to my academic expectations, waiting at home for years to gain admission into school, and many other things. However, I didn't give up on my dreams. But I was clear about what I wanted, and I knew that the only way I could obtain it was by putting in a lot of effort, remaining consistent, believing in myself, and not giving up.

Although there were many distractions that could have caused me to give up on my goals, I was confident in my capacity to achieve success, provided that I gave it sufficient time and effort. Even when I was slipping farther and farther behind in school and my friend was already a long way ahead of me, I did not lose my patience. In general, I remained faithful, and I clung to the belief that everything would work out for the best.

There is no justifiable excuse for throwing in the towel on your chosen course and future. If you talk to enough people, some of them will tell you that they regret not being able to put away more money when they were younger because they either did not have somebody to advise them on how to do so or they chose to disregard the guidance that was offered to them.

You will be able to view this page, so there is no reason to give up right now, at this very moment! There is no justification for failure; hence, you must learn to cope with the unease in the here and now in order to have something to offer the rest of the world in the future. You are setting yourself up for failure in the future if you choose to dismiss any of the lessons that life has to offer right now.

Whatever you plant now will produce a harvest tomorrow, so it is important to give great consideration to the kinds of outcomes you would like to see. What you are doing at this very moment is the initial step in determining the answer. If I was able to get through those difficult times, then you can do it, too. Absolutely nothing can be ruled out as a possibility. Don't throw in the towel until you've realized your full potential, whether that means becoming an extremely successful person or something else entirely. You can succeed where I've failed since I'm living proof of that fact. Always shoot for the stars, and don't throw in the towel until you've reached the pinnacle of achievement. The journey that is life is not an easy one.

In the majority of situations, it calls for an amount of effort that appears to be insurmountable. No matter how vulnerable we are or how we feel about the challenges we face, life will continue to present us with obstacles that appear insurmountable. Those who can get back up when things go wrong and keep going after their goals no matter what will be rewarded in this life.

No matter how difficult it is or how exhausted you feel, you must not give up. Keep in mind that achieving your objectives will require a significant investment of time, effort, dedication, and sacrifice on your part. This is because as long as you are still living, you have a greater degree of power over your own life than you may realize.

There is, therefore, no basis for giving up at this point. There are going to be people in your life who will attempt to dissuade you from following your heart. They will tell you that what you want to accomplish is not possible in any way, shape, or form. Having said that, you are aware that there is a bigger purpose for your existence. You have a solid understanding of the fantastic things you are capable of doing and the potential that is within you. Therefore, use their criticism as fuel to propel you forward in your endeavours. Those are wise words to live by. Your hopes, wishes, ambitions, and desires shouldn't be given up so easily. I will continue to stress the idea that if I can accomplish something, so can you.

CHAPTER 11

POWER OF DISCIPLINE

This chapter shows you how to develop the self-discipline and mental toughness you need to be successful.

How would you react if I told you that the reason you aren't successful isn't that you lack motivation or are lazy, but because you were never taught how to practise self-discipline? How would you react to that?

Self-control is not an intrinsic quality; rather, it is acquired through experience and training. It is a skill that can be learned, just like operating a motor vehicle or serving a tennis ball. Strategies for enhancing the capacities of the areas of the brain that are accountable for self-control

Self-discipline techniques used by world leaders and military methods of control and order implemented over decades, bringing a sense of humour to strenuous work, and learning the routines of those who have attained greatness will assist you in kicking your destructive routines and making other positive changes in your life. You should use these tactics when you feel your motivation beginning to wane.

In addition to a considerable number of other things, make use of the instructions contained in this chapter to hone your self-control and habits, charge headfirst at your aspirations, change into an unstoppable force, and give yourself the life that you are aware you deserve. Even though you can't reverse what's happened in the past, you can affect what happens in the future.

Exercise of Self-Control and Perseverance in One's Work Until It Is Accomplished

"That mountain is too big for you to ever reach the top; the only way you can genuinely win the struggle against your own mind is by accepting responsibility for your own acts."

Allan Mandindi

Discipline is a distinct form of inner motivation. A mix of internal desire, a strong will, a readiness to take action, and the discipline to see a task through to its conclusion are the components that contribute to the development of self-discipline.

Why is it important to exercise self-control, and what are the benefits? The practise of discipline is beneficial in many aspects of our lives. Example: It's what makes you keep working hard even when you don't feel like it. If you maintain this mindset, you will be able to continue professionally interacting with consumers even when you feel like throwing in the towel. When things get rough, it pushes you to keep going, which is crucial to achieving the goals that you have set for yourself. You can achieve tremendous success by pushing through challenges that, to others, may appear to be insurmountable, thanks to the aid that discipline provides.

In addition, there are positive effects on performance and academics. Students who exercise high levels of self-discipline are more likely to be able to remember what they have learned, according to research. This is in contrast to students who do not practise self-discipline. Researchers also discovered that students who had higher degrees of self-discipline completed their assignments with greater care, which resulted in higher grade point averages. Studies have shown that a person's level of self-discipline can be a more reliable indicator of future success than a person's IQ.

Discover how to be disciplined right now!

In the same way that a muscle may be built through exercise and training, self-discipline can also be strengthened in this way. Nevertheless, it is of the utmost importance to refrain from beginning with unreasonable expectations. Instead, you should begin with objectives that are easily attainable and progressively increase the level of difficulty. You will make progress if you are willing to put in the necessary time and effort. Try out these steps as a means of getting started on the road to increased self-control:

- Choosing a target is the first thing to do. Choose one aspect of self-discipline that you feel needs improvement and focus all of your attention and energy on that for a little while. If you want to improve your abilities, maybe you should start reading a leadership book once a week, or maybe you should start working out every night. Both of these things can help. Self-discipline can be practised with even the smallest of goals, such as refraining from eating unhealthy food for an entire day or concentrating on a single task for an entire hour without checking your messages. Both of these examples are good ways to get started.

The first thing you should do if you want to gain self-discipline is to do things slowly and methodically. As your capacity for self-control grows, you'll be able to apply it to an increasing number of challenging situations. If you want to be successful, you need to make sure that the goals you set are SMART, which stands for specific, measurable, attainable, relevant, and time-bound. Additionally, you need to create sub-goals whenever it is possible to do so.

- Find Your Parking Space: When you have decided on a goal, it is beneficial to write down all of the aspects that will ultimately contribute to the achievement of that goal. Make an effort to present your reasoning in a positive light by trying to frame it as such. Consider saying something like, "I want to complete this assignment so that I may achieve my goals, earn praise from my supervisor, and feel pleased with the job that I did today" as an alternative to saying, "I want to check this item off my To-Finish List." One of the most effective ways to motivate yourself to finish a task is to write down the reasons you want to accomplish it.

- Recognise the obstacles you face. The next thing you need to do is think ahead to the difficulties that may arise as you work towards your goal and plan a strategy to achieve it that will allow you to tackle each one head-on. Assume for a moment that you are interested in enhancing your leadership skills and have settled on the goal of reading one book every week. In the past, you had to triumph over a lot of challenges in order to be successful in this endeavour. When you have searched high and low for a book that you can truly get lost in, it might be difficult to carve out enough time in your schedule each evening to read it. Because you are so busy with work, school, dinner, and the children, you simply do not have the time to read. After locating each issue, devise a strategy for how you intend to address it and put it into action. Using the preceding instance as an example, the following are some options open to you: Create more time in your schedule so that you can read. Reading is something you may do while waiting for your children to arrive home from school or while you are eating lunch. Put away your phone if you want to read in peace. You won't be able to concentrate otherwise. Instead of letting social media tell you how to spend your time, make a schedule for when you will interact with it. To put it another way, you need to stop allowing time to govern you. Because we haven't thought ahead and prepared for the difficulties that lie ahead of us, we are unable to sustain our self-discipline. Our self-assurance is suffering as a direct result of our inadequate preparation to meet these problems should they materialise.

- Eliminating the use of outdated methods Developing self-control typically involves abandoning unwanted behaviours in favour of those that are more suited to our needs. If the habit is inextricably related to a specific time of day or daily routine, the void that it leaves behind may be more noticeable. If we don't find another activity to take its place, the lack of that habit will be felt more keenly than it otherwise would be. One good example would be to resist the urge to do some online shopping over lunch rather than giving in to it. If you routinely spend twenty to thirty minutes at a time online, you will notice a significant decline in your capacity to concentrate and focus on a single task. When you have made the decision to stop smoking, it can be helpful to think of an alternative activity that you can do whenever you feel the need for a little break from your typical routine. You may choose to stretch at your workplace, take a cup of coffee, or go for a brief walk outside rather than engage in any online shopping. Your break will not be wasted if you engage in these activities because they will assist you in reaching your objective and foster greater self-discipline.

- Maintain a close watch on your progress. Pay close attention to the changes in your mood as your self-discipline improves and becomes more robust as you continue to exercise it. It is probable that you will have a reawakened sense of vitality, pride, joy, and independence after achieving your goal. You might want to keep a journal in which you document your strategies for improving your self-control and the actions you take to bring those strategies to fruition. This will help to reinforce the changes in lifestyle that you are making and will provide a record of your accomplishments in the future. Your capacity for self-control will improve with the passage of time. In addition, it will be helpful for a number of purposes. It is essential that you do not allow yourself to be disrupted while you are practising self-control. Make it more challenging to engage in the activity that you do not want. It is essential to celebrate one's success with a party whenever a target has been attained. Keeping yourself motivated to carry on with your efforts will be easier if you celebrate and enjoy your victories. You shouldn't allow the possibility of failing or a brief setback to get you down or dampen your enthusiasm. Everyone will, at some point in their lives, experience both success and failure. Accept that you were wrong, evaluate how you might become a better person, and then move on. The capacity to exert one's own self-control is absolutely necessary. The ability to exercise self-control is essential to delivering professional results. This motivates us to keep striving towards our goals, even when things get difficult. In addition to this, it helps us maintain our professionalism even on days when we aren't feeling quite up to par. The following are some pointers to consider when exercising the muscle of self-control: Pick one thing out of all the things you wish to achieve. Make an effort to find some motivation. acquire the ability to identify difficulties. Get out of the rut you're in. Be careful to keep an eye on how far you've progressed. Self-discipline is one of the most important qualities, and it is a significant factor in determining who succeeds in life and who does not. Some people have it, while others do not. The patterns of conduct that people develop, often unknowingly, determine the way they go about their daily lives. It's not uncommon for people to try to kick undesirable habits by simply applying more of their willpower, but this strategy almost never works. Studies have shown that these are the most effective techniques for developing new routines that are beneficial to one's life. You've made the decision to alter some aspects of your day-to-day routine, such as the amount of time you spend exercising, your level of productivity at work, or the acquisition of a new skill. You make the decision to carry it out, gather up your resolve, and then actually do it. You, however, are one of the vast majority of people who will eventually be unsuccessful. Our lives are moulded by our habits.

The routines that we get into become the foundation upon which our lives are built, and most of the time, we don't even realise it. Humans do possess evolved brains that are capable of creative thinking, problem-solving, and strategic planning. However, the majority of how we spend our time and energy can be attributed to the routines that we engage in daily. These are the actions that we carry out without giving them much thought. The majority of the things we do each day are habits. Because of this, it is important to take a good look at our habits and determine whether or not they are contributing positively or negatively to our lives.

What do we mean when we talk about habits? Automatic behaviours are referred to as "habits." They are triggered in reaction to environmental cues such as time of day or location, rather than needing intentional action on the part of the individual. Your brain creates a connection between a particular setting and a particular action through the process of associative learning. After that, you automatically engage in that pattern of conduct, whether it be a ritual or a habit, when you are in that situation. The act of checking email as soon as one arrives at work in the morning, travelling the same path home every evening, gnawing one's fingernails when anxious, or reading through one's social media newsfeed just before getting into bed at night are all examples of habits.

How do routines come to be? When the brain receives stimulation from anything pleasurable, dopamine, a neurotransmitter, enters the bloodstream. Because this "dopamine rush" makes you feel good, you are encouraged to continue engaging in that behaviour so that you can be rewarded with more dopamine in the future.

Your brain's basal ganglia and dorsolateral striatum, both of which are associated with feelings and implicit learning, are the locations in which the association between context, behaviour, and reward is stored over time. This happens over time. For instance, perusing your newsfeed late at night could be fun, at least on occasion. Therefore, without even realising it, the expectation of getting another hit of dopamine causes you to check it again right before you go to bed. After some time, this pattern will get ingrained in your brain, making it difficult to break.

Habits endure even when rewards end. Some behaviours might become so established over time that they continue even after the reward is no longer available. It is rare for knowledge, strategy, or effort alone to be sufficient to change habits. Keep in mind that the basal ganglia and the dorsolateral striatum are the parts of the brain that are responsible for storing habits. Emotion and procedural memory, such as how to ride a bike or perform other actions, are both controlled by these regions of the brain. These regions are also involved in basic life functions. They are seen as being somewhat rudimentary, or even primal, as they developed early on in the course of evolution to ensure that animals fulfilled the "Four Fs": feeding, fighting, fleeing, and reproducing. On the other hand, the prefrontal cortex is primarily responsible for controlling things like self-control, explicit knowledge (such as the ability to express facts), and planning. The most developed portion of the human brain is called the prefrontal cortex. However, this location is distinct from the one where habits are saved. It is a way of securing the most important information and protecting it from change. Our routines are stored in a memory system that we do not have access to and are unable to manipulate.

What are some ways to alter habits? Make a new habit. To summarise, developing a new routine is the most effective strategy for breaking an old one. This indicates that you are required to accomplish a new behaviour in a specific setting, obtain a reward, and then repeat the process. Of course, saying something is simpler than actually doing it. Because of what psychologists refer to as "friction," the process of forming new habits can be difficult. Friction refers to the obstacles that stand in the way of completing a behaviour, such as distance, time, and effort.

Develop a supportive setting. The creation of an environment that facilitates the new habit in a way that is both simple and rewarding is one of the most effective strategies to reduce friction. It is hoped that the new environment will reduce the number of old cues that led to harmful habits while simultaneously increasing the number of cues that lead to positive new habits.

When trying to modify behaviours, one of the most important things to keep in mind is that you have to work with the environment around you. We are in desperate need of an atmosphere that would make it simpler for us to accomplish our objectives. Utilise your routines to your advantage. Even though they have a bad reputation, habits, when used correctly, can significantly improve one's quality of life. Your life can gain a sense of structure, control, and even significance when you develop healthy habits, in addition to assisting you in accomplishing your goals. For example, many elite athletes find that engaging in particular rituals either before or during competition helps them feel more in control of their bodies and minds. Some people may have rituals or customs in their families that hold significant value for them. However, even the most mundane routines can be beneficial. Because habits require such a small amount of mental effort, they can also free up your attention to focus on other things, such as considering your significant life goals or giving your mother a call as you are driving home. After we've had sufficient practise with something, at which point we won't need to worry about it anymore, we can go on to other things.

Self-discipline. Let's be honest. Most of us are still working on it, and it is full of feelings of not being good enough, being slow, and having good intentions. But that isn't necessarily the case. Practise is necessary for everything, including developing self-discipline. Every day will not go according to plan, but even with its share of setbacks and accomplishments, each day represents growth, which is the point of practising self-discipline in the first place.

What exactly does "self-discipline" mean? Self-discipline can be defined as the ability to act in accordance with one's own best interests. In order to achieve long-term success, it is often necessary to sacrifice short-term comfort or desires in favour of exercising self-discipline. For instance, if you want to improve your physical fitness, you might be willing to put up with the temporary unpleasantness of getting up at 5:00 in the morning and spending time in the gym so that you might enjoy the fruits of good health and contentment farther down the road in your body. Simply put, our emotional minds prevent us from behaving in the way that is necessary for us to reach our optimum state. The capacity to exercise self-discipline grants us the power to triumph over our emotional minds by allowing us to move on with physical activity.

There are several benefits that come along with cultivating self-discipline, one of which is the ability to advance in one's job. It's been shown to be beneficial to several people: The development of self-discipline, which enables people to suppress short-term desires in favour of more important long-term objectives, makes the achievement of long-term objectives possible.

As a person who has served in the British Armed Forces in the past, I am eligible to say that if I can do it, so can you. I was born in Malawi's largest and most important city, Lilongwe. I am the oldest child in my family of seven, which consists of four boys and three girls. Although there are now only six left because one of my younger brothers was killed in a car accident, my parents both spent their careers up until their retirement working in the public sector as civil servants. Being the eldest child in my family has always made me feel as though I have a tremendous amount of duty to carry with me wherever I go.

Have you been putting in effort for a number of days, months, or even years but to no avail? Have you given up on accomplishing your objectives because you believe that success is only possible for a select few individuals?

If you answered "yes" to any of these questions, there is still a chance that things will work out for you. To have any chance of being successful in life, you need to first train yourself to have a high level of self-discipline. The innate talent, intelligence, or skill of an individual only accounts for half of the picture. Only a piece of the solution entails the use of affirmations, vision boards, and other forms of optimistic thought processes. If you want to make your dreams come true, exercising self-control is really necessary. When everything seems to be falling apart and you are on the verge of failing, self-discipline is what helps you keep going when you feel like giving up. Your resolve will be strengthened, and you will be able to break down the boundaries that you have put on yourself and overcome any obstacles that stand in your way.

The United Kingdom is where I first became acquainted with my lovely Jamaican wife, and since then, we have been blessed with two children: a boy and a girl. I am now happily married to her. My father is originally from a rural area of Lilongwe, which is the capital city of Malawi. This area is known as Kasiya, and it is under the traditional authority of Khongoni. My father has always wished for me to be celebrated in this area just like him and to be able to help people. This is an area in which, up to this point, there have only been a small number of people who are educated and successful. Even though I was brought up in a family that had the financial means to provide for all of our needs, I struggled emotionally in school because I was unable to meet the expectations that my parents had set for me.

This made my life more difficult than it should have been. Despite the fact that my academic performance was less than stellar and that it was challenging for me to imagine what kind of person I would like to be in the future, I never gave up. The most excruciating part was that whenever you went home to visit family, the first question they asked was what your class number was. Because of the humiliating nature of my position in the class, I did my best to steer clear of conversations of this nature whenever possible. Despite this, I had faith in myself since I was aware that there was some aspect of my life in which I excelled, but it was up to me to discover what it was.

When I was in elementary school, I was not the brightest kid you could meet, but I always had the desire to study more, so I would consider myself to have been an average student. During the primary school examination that I was taking at our school, Chilambula, there was a rumour going around that the school had passed with a perfect score. This caused the examination board to raise an eyebrow, and as a result, the entire school was disqualified. When I heard the news, it hurt my heart because my father could not accept the justification, and he blamed me for failing since I had been careless and mischievous.

No matter how I attempted to defend myself in front of my loved ones and friends, I was simply another loser. The failed cap caused me a lot of discomfort wherever I went, and I had to wear it. My parents decided to send me to a school called Kamzimbi, which is a self-boarding school located in my father's home village of Kasiya. They intended for me to repeat the eighth standard there. At that time, the majority of my acquaintances and their parents enrolled them in private schools from the very beginning of their education. This caused a great deal of agony. This left me in a very damaged state and gave me a lot of negative thoughts, one of which was that my father did not love or care about me. I had no idea that the experience I was about to have at that village school would change the way I think about things and make me a better person for the rest of my life.

Never in a million years did I imagine that it would. When the time came to leave, fortunately, I was informed that I would not be travelling alone on this adventure. My lifelong friend Collins, who lived next door to me and was my best friend in elementary school, was supposed to accompany me because we were both in the same position; nevertheless, we were both unsuccessful. We set out on the dusty roads of Kasiya, and we arrived in the evening. It was very dark as the entire village lacked any form of electricity, but the stars helped us easily see the faces of those who greeted us when we arrived. The rumour of our arrival spread throughout the community, and our guide led us to the dwelling that would be ours for the next year—a grass-thatched, round mud cottage with nothing more than a mat on the interior.

The following day, we were prepared to begin our education. The school that we attended was a typical neighbourhood school. We found out that it was well-known in the region due to its excellent track record in terms of pass rate and the fact that the teachers devoted themselves to offering self-boarding to students, the majority of whom travelled quite a distance to attend the school. The teachers were so passionate about their jobs that they offered to do all of these for free.

At the time, Collins and I were the only two boys from town who stayed in this area. We were given very respectful treatment, and we had no trouble getting along with the rest of the students and villagers. The majority of the villagers referred to us as town boys, and they were eager to make friends with us. My manner of thinking and the perspective I had on life were both significantly altered as a result of this encounter.

Regardless of the circumstances you could find yourself in, if you have the ability to flip a negative scenario into a positive one, everything will shift. There are times when we find ourselves in situations in which we believe that it is the end of us, but in reality, it may be the beginning of a new version of us. When we went back to repeat a class at this village school, some of our friends who attended private schools laughed at us for doing so.

When we go back to our hometown for the holidays, we often have to hide because we do not want to see our private school friends. Neither of us realised that God had something entirely different in store for us. Things that occur throughout our lives serve the purpose of preparing us for something that lies ahead. The education I received at that school is directly responsible for my development into the person I am now as well as my accomplishments in the community, regardless of what I choose to do. Because of all we went through, we are now unique individuals in comparison to everyone else.

Today, people who I previously felt were ahead of us and had attended universities are questioning me about how I was able to achieve what I have. The solution is that we need to start thinking positively all the time and outside the box in order to maximise our potential. In life, you shouldn't just blindly imitate what other people are doing; we need to be able to transform negativity into positivity. If people make fun of you because of who you are now, you should not be concerned about the future since only God knows what it holds. If you strive to be the best at whatever it is that you do, in the end, you will obtain what you want, you will become an expert, and you may even be able to establish your own business and hire other people. Everyone has the potential for greatness, but it is up to them to discover what they are good at and work to improve those skills. According to the principle known as the "law of attraction," in life, you will attract whatever you give your attention to.

Whatever you focus your time, discipline, and effort on will have a greater chance of becoming a reality for you. Find out what it is that you want to become, then get to work and start moving in that direction; eventually, people will begin to identify you with it. Negativity does not produce anything constructive; rather, it destroys, and if we are not strong enough to combat it, it can even push people to end their own lives. We went to the village, but we took it as an opportunity, as we attracted attention that we couldn't get in town and learned to understand and value people. Building a positive mindset and seeing every situation as an opportunity is something you should do. something that, in the long run, proved to be helpful and set me apart from others.

Despite having earned a passing grade in the primary school exam given at the village school, I was not chosen for the secondary school programme offered by the government. I received my secondary education at a prestigious private institution in northern Malawi. This was one of the best schools, and it's where I finished Form 4 and did well enough to meet the minimum requirement of six credits to enter Malawi University.

However, because of the high number of students who graduated that year, admission to Malawi University was not guaranteed.

The government made the decision that students should take entrance exams while applying to universities. When the list of individuals who had been chosen was revealed, you would not have seen my name on it. This was another setback in my life, and at the time, I thought it was the end of me. I also began to view myself as a failure as a result of this. I was able to watch as several of my friends made progress towards being chosen to attend Malawi University. There wasn't much hope for me, but then I saw an advertisement for a position open at the Malawi Intelligence Agency in the local paper. The agency was looking to hire students who had completed six credits. I applied, but when I showed up for the interviews, I found out that it was rigged in some way, as the majority of the students that were present had relatives working in the ministry that supervised the agency.

The news that I had not been chosen did not come as a surprise to me, but it did cause my parents to become increasingly concerned about my future. During that period in my neighbourhood, there were a few people who passed with great grades but were doing nothing, and they just ended up being seen as useless because they were just staying at home with their parents. These people were the exception, however, as the majority of the people in my neighbourhood failed. I had no intention of becoming a member of this group. At that time, there were not many people in our culture who could serve as examples for us to look up to and say that they had achieved success in life without going through the traditional channels of scholastic achievement. However, I never gave up; I continued researching and exploring different subjects because I believed that no matter what challenges we face in life, we all have a purpose in life that we are meant to fulfil. My goal was to one day become a writer and then one day become the mayor of my hometown, Lilongwe. A door opened up in the United Kingdom since only a handful of colleges were advertising in Malawi through their respective agents. Emile Woolf College was one of these colleges, and they were providing accounting training at the time. I was never excellent in arithmetic or accounting, but I saw this as a tremendous opportunity to get away from the stigma of being dependent on my parents for the rest of my life, as other people did. After finishing my secondary education at Phwezi Private School, After finishing my secondary education at Phwezi Private School in the north of Malawi, I moved to the United Kingdom on March 15, 2003. This was after I had completed my education in Malawi.

Despite the fact that I had a strong academic record, I was not accepted into the university of my choice. Coming to the United Kingdom was really difficult for me because I had no idea what I was getting myself into, and no one was there for me like they were back home. Yet I viewed coming here as a second chance for myself. When I was still in the beginning stages of my studies at Emile Woolf, I came to the conclusion that accounting was not the right major for me. Not only was I having difficulty passing certain modules, but the higher international student fees imposed on international students were also causing me to waste money. Even though my father was helping to partially sponsor me, I had to give it up since I could no longer afford it. Every time I had to apply for a visa valid for six months, which was incredibly expensive, I started to run into problems with the visa. I vowed to myself that I would not make the same mistake twice, especially because I had no one else to turn to for assistance. I've made the decision to just put all of my energy into finding a job and increasing my savings so that if my visa application is denied, at least I'll have something to take with me when I go back home. When I was about to leave Malawi, my mother gave me some sound advice that helped me prepare for the trip.

One day, as I was sitting down and looking at my passport, I noticed that there were not many days left. She gave me a verse from Isaiah 54:17, which said, "No weapon fashioned against you shall prosper," and she added, "My son, any land you set foot in, pray and declare it as your home," and this was a prayer I did. Then, as if by some act of divine intervention, a buddy of mine who was serving in the British Army came to see me. He raved about the British Army to me and said that serving in the military offered a wide variety of chances, including the chance to further one's education. It wasn't hard to convince me to sign up for the British Army. Surprisingly, it also occurred during that same week that they were looking for new employees in Manchester. I went to the Army recruitment centre in Manchester city centre, and that was the beginning of something new in my life as well as another significant turning point. I joined the Army. It was difficult to relay my decision to my parents; they did not take it well because they believed I was going to die and also because they believed that this could be the end of any chance I had of achieving my academic dream. Everyone shared the opinion that having one's child join the military was not a desirable path, particularly given the state of affairs in Afghanistan at the moment. Every day, all that was reported in the press was the death of another British soldier serving in Afghanistan. I enlisted in 2008 and went on to train as a supplier specialist with the Royal Logistics Corps. I completed my basic training at Bassingbourn, which is located in the southern part of the United Kingdom, and I completed my specialist training at Defence Logistics school, Deepcut. During the five years that I spent serving in the army, I made some of the best friends I will ever have. It was the best time of my life. At that time, I was stationed in Germany for a period of three years and served as a member of the ammunition squadron at the 6th Supply Regiment, which had its headquarters in Gutersloh. There, I was chosen to be a member of the team that would represent my squadron on operational tours in Afghanistan lasting six months each, during which we would provide logistical supply and support to other infantry regiments located in that country. 2011 was the year that the tour of duty came to a conclusion, and for the exceptional work that we did, each of us was presented with the Afghanistan Service Medal.

Why do I have such a long list of successes, and why do I keep getting lucky when I try to do things? And what are some ways that you, in your own life and professional efforts, might make progress comparable to what has been made here? The approach relies heavily on the individual's capacity for self-control. This is what drives us to pursue our loftiest goals even on days when we don't feel like it, even if we know it's the right thing to do. With self-discipline, we are able to postpone the gratification of a fleeting need and endure the discomfort and hardship of the here and now for the benefit of our long-term enjoyment. Because of this, having good self-control is absolutely necessary. In this chapter, we are going to look at self-discipline in great detail, exploring what it is, why it is important, and how it may be developed. and walk you through several procedures that will prove to be helpful.

While we were at Camp Bastion, Prince Harry and his team were also stationed there, and we were able to spot them in the dining hall. After receiving an acceptance letter from Manchester Metropolitan University and a scholarship from the Army to pursue a degree in political science there, I decided to leave the army in 2013. I was overcome with emotion since I had been looking forward to doing this for a very long time. I kept pushing myself and continued to take other classes as I worked towards my goal of enrolling in the Political Science programme at Manchester Metropolitan University. 2017 marked the year of my graduation with a BA with honours. A year later, in 2018, I received my master's degree in international relations and global communication. Before that, I studied politics. None of this took place by itself. In order to fulfil my lifelong goal of earning a degree, I had to put in a lot of effort. After some time, I realised that this was a subject in which I excelled, even more so than accounting. Already on a daily basis, I was looking through the political news articles in the newspaper to get an idea of what was going on in Malawi and elsewhere in the world. No matter how challenging life may be, we all have something within us that we excel at, and it is up to us to find out what that is so that we can realise our full potential. It took me some time to figure out what it was that I was good at. It's possible that the things we do on a regular basis, even when we're not aware of them, are the very activities that require the most attention and effort from us in order to become proficient in them.

Despite the fact that I wasn't the smartest student in the class, I was always good at managing people. Whenever I got involved in a group, I was always selected to be the leader, and I never hesitated to accept the offer when it was presented to me. This is due to the fact that I began to comprehend my capabilities and strengths. My time spent in both the hamlet and the army helped me develop the manner in which I carry myself, which ultimately led to my recognition. It is imperative that we evaluate both our capabilities and our shortcomings in order to make the necessary improvements. Even though I was in the middle of the 80 students in my primary school class, I was given the responsibility of being the monitor. I was a typical student in secondary school, but my teachers singled me out as exceptional and worked with me to improve. When I got to university, I was elected as the class representative and given a seat on the school committee to represent my fellow students. After that, I decided that my calling was to serve the public in some way, whether as an elected official or an appointed official. I started to push myself and get better, taking advantage of every chance to get the skills, experience, and education I would need for such a job.

During the time that I have been living in the United Kingdom, I was one of the people who founded and established the Malawi Congress Party Diaspora Network and became the Global Network's first vice chairperson and chair of the United Kingdom wing. Now the network has grown massively and is well established as a global network of professionals that advise the party and government. The Malawi Congress Party is the largest political party in Malawi, and the Diaspora organisations have contributed hugely to the development of Malawi. The network now has branches in the United States of America, Dubai, South Africa, Kenya, Ireland, Zimbabwe, and Canada and continues to expand. In 2018, soon after we officially established the network, I visited Malawi on another business trip, and I was granted the opportunity to meet the president of the party, Dr. Lazarus Chakwera, who at that time was the leader of the opposition. During our meeting, I persuaded him to come to the UK, specifically Manchester, to meet the members of the newly established network, and this happened the same year. This trip was a turning point. It enhanced the support and helped increase diaspora engagement. My political knowledge really helped me point the network in the right direction. I have always used my politics and diplomacy to negotiate on behalf of my community. The networks' support in 2019 and 2020 contributed massively to the election of President Chakwera as Malawi's 6th President, and this is something I will always be proud of. The president has been a great inspiration. I joined the Labour Party during my university days in Manchester and met a lot of student activists who encouraged me to get involved in local community activities and stand up for people. I got myself involved with the local Labour Party, and I was elected to the position of Vice-Chairperson of the Openshaw branch. In 2016, I was invited to join the Malawian Diaspora organisation Maravi Heritage Foundation, which is now known as Malawi Heritage, as a co-founder. Through this organisation, we have collaborated with a wide variety of communities in Malawi. We began our land preservation initiative, known as "One Tree, One Citizen," in 2018, and by the end of the year, we had planted almost 200,000 trees. For our efforts, we were presented with an award by Trumpet Media Group at the annual Gathering of Africa's Best event. In addition to that, I've been volunteering my time with a number of different organisations and communities in Manchester, and because of the good impact that I've had there, Greatness University has honoured me with the titles of Creator of Greatness and World Civility Ambassador.

The United Graduate College and Seminary International in the United States of America bestowed upon me an honorary doctorate of philosophy in the field of humanities in the year 2023. This distinction is a reflection of my commitment and the hard work I've put into encouraging youth and civility leadership, reaching nations through my books and online, and having an impact in many different places.

In addition to that, Charisma has put my name in consideration for the Manchester Peace Award. All of these accomplishments come from a person who, at one point in their life, believed that the world had nothing else to offer. We don't need to wait for change because we are the change; all we need to do is take the first step towards making that change happen. We don't need to wait for change because we are the change.

What exactly does it mean to have self-control? Discipline entails actively pushing oneself to make forward progress, maintaining one's own motivation, and acting in spite of one's emotional state. You exhibit persistence whenever you make the deliberate decision to better yourself in spite of challenges such as a lack of time, boredom, or opposition. Willpower and other forms of inner motivation are not the same thing as discipline.

Do not surrender under any circumstances; if I was able to overcome this obstacle, then you, too, can overcome this obstacle. I just learned that kids who improve their ability to exercise self-control may find it easier to manage anxiety-related issues during standardised testing. People who are more self-disciplined are less likely to do things that are bad for their health, like smoking cigarettes or drinking too much alcohol.

This is probably something you already knew. There is a correlation between having self-control and reducing obesity and addiction rates. Self-discipline can also have a beneficial effect on one's relationships, contributing to their overall improvement. Psychologists have concluded that the ability to exert self-control is linked to the ability to empathise with others and see things from their perspective. By using these measures, we may learn to control our habitual defensive responses and replace them with those that strengthen our relationships and improve our quality of life. Develop your resilience. Are you able to quickly get back on your feet after experiencing a setback? The ability to exercise self-control can be a useful indicator of resilience. It would appear that the more resilient a person is, the more control they have over their impulses and their ability to defer gratification.

According to psychologists, a resilient person has a belief in her own skills to effectively manage the obstacles and situations that life presents. Your level of happiness and creativity will increase in direct proportion to the amount of work you get done. When we have a better sense of well-being and happiness, it's because we have more control over the factors that contribute to the origin of our behaviour.

A Guide to Building Your Own Self-Discipline:

- Understand where your weaknesses and strengths are.
- Determine and document your exact objectives.
- Imagine how things will turn out.

- Don't hold off until it "feels right" to act.
- Start small
- Look for a role model.
- Practise, make mistakes, and then begin again.
- Know how you'll evaluate your advancement.
- Be mindful of your own well-being.
- Give yourself a reward.
- Forgive yourself
- Learn about your own areas of weakness. Make a list of everything you do on an average day to get started. The second stage is to think about what you value and whether or not your present action reflects it. You undoubtedly have some practises that you indulge in regularly that go against those principles (we are all flawed individuals because we are all humans). During the identification phase, the people who are closest to us, such as our family, our mentors, and our coworkers, may give us valuable comments. Take a look at how others evaluate your shortcomings and how you see them in yourself to see if there is any consistency between the two. As soon as you've zoomed in on a few areas that require improvement, build a strategy to tackle them. One of your shortcomings may be that you procrastinate calling potential customers until the end of the

business day, at which point it is too late. This has put me off schedule for the remainder of the week, making it tough to accomplish my objective. The moment I walk through the door at work tomorrow, the first thing I'm going to do is pick up the phone and make a call.

- Find out how you can be successful. You may get things rolling by saying hello to your colleagues and asking them how their evenings are going. If you would like coffee, the best place to get it is in the kitchen. The amount of lost productivity that accumulates over the course of a workweek due to activities like team lunches and visits to local coffee shops is substantial. These types of activities take place outside of the workplace. Every occupation necessitates the taking of frequent breaks, both mentally and physically, as well as the formation of interpersonal relationships with one's fellow employees. However, it is critical that you be open and honest about the procedures you used to organise your work. If you often waste your mornings on activities that have nothing to do with your company, this is not a particularly encouraging sign that you have put your job low on your list of priorities. Adjust your schedule so that it revolves around the times of day when you are most productive. In the event that you spend most of your time in the area between the hours of 9 a.m. and 3 p.m. Coffee breaks with your staff should take place between the hours of noon and one o'clock in the afternoon. You may improve your chances of professional success while lowering the hazards involved. By doing so, you will be contributing to the development of an atmosphere that is beneficial to you on a personal level and fruitful for the company.

- Determine and document your exact objectives. Did you know that writing down your goals increases the likelihood that you will accomplish them? The process of writing down goals compels you to imagine not just the goal but also the means by which it can be accomplished and the sequence of actions that must be taken to reach it. Consequently, before you embark on a journey to become the best version of yourself, either in business or in your personal life, you should first determine your objectives and document them.

- Imagine how things will turn out. Your brain is unable to discern between true memories and those that you have fabricated. Therefore, the brain's chemical composition changes in the same way as if you had truly experienced the event you are imagining in exquisite detail. If you're feeling insecure about your chances of making it to the top of the activity board, giving yourself positive self-talk like "When I make it to the top of our activity board, I'm going to treat myself to an exquisite meal" will help. As a consequence, you'll find it less challenging to push past your fears and take the necessary steps towards realising your goals.

- Don't hold off until it "feels right" to act. It is possible that you will never get started on the job that needs to be done if you wait until your schedule is ideal, your workspace is devoid of clutter, or your inbox has reached a level that is manageable. Embrace every moment as though it already possesses exactly what you require to perform at your best, because, well, it does.

- Start small. Do you find that this list motivates you in any way? Have you given any thought to the possibility of becoming the perfect employee or salesman and whether or not you already have the capacity to do so? Begin by taking tiny steps. If you think you can completely change your approach to work in one week, you are setting yourself up for feelings of frustration and exhaustion. Instead, focus on developing a handful of simple behaviours that you can work on improving on a weekly basis. If you want to get a head start on your job and avoid the early distractions that are referred to as "the break room," you might wish to bring your own coffee to the office during the first week. This will allow you to get a head start on your work. If you've had a productive week, the afternoon on Friday is a great time to catch up on administrative work such as making notes on prospects and responding to any unread emails you may have. You might be surprised at how much more disciplined and productive you have become after focusing on changing only one behaviour at a time for a few weeks.

- Look for a role model. There are topics that you are free to talk about with a mentor but might not feel comfortable approaching with a coworker or management. If I want to avoid upsetting my boss, I think it would be best to address the necessity of spending less time on social media in favour of prospecting alongside my mentor. For example, if I want to stop wasting so much time on social media when I'm supposed to be prospecting, mentors typically have more experience than their mentees, have a strong familiarity with them, and are able to provide the candid guidance and feedback that mentees require to achieve success, not just in their current jobs but also throughout their careers.

- Exercise, make mistakes, and then begin again. It's not that people who have self-discipline never have days where they eat all of the doughnuts in the kitchen, spend 45 minutes on social media, and lose two prospects before 10:00 a.m. What it means is that self-disciplined people have days where they eat all of the doughnuts in the kitchen. The problem is that when individuals act in this manner, they try to improve their judgement the next day by choosing differently. The act of trying something, being unsuccessful at it, and then trying it again is the essence of self-discipline.

- Determine how you will measure your level of success. It will be impossible to determine whether or not you are successful if you do not have a plan for how you will track your progress. If increasing the number of meetings you book during the first half of the month is one of your objectives, the first step is to determine how many meetings you want to book. The next step is to perform a reverse calculation to determine how many meetings you will require each week and how long each one will take to complete. After you have worked out the specifics of your objective, the next step is to define what constitutes a successful outcome. Are you primarily concerned with the total score? Will it make a difference if we cancel a meeting at the very last minute? Should a presentation be given at the meeting? You must first define what success looks like in order to understand how to quantify it.

- Be mindful of your well-being. If you torture yourself in order to develop more self-discipline, your efforts will be for naught. Burning the midnight oil for weeks or months on end in an effort to be more "self-disciplined" is missing the point. Everyone works a 28-hour day once in a while (you know those exist, right?), but if that's how you spend most of your time, you're missing the boat. Self-care is an important component of developing self-discipline. The planet and all of us need to take regular breaks during the day, maintain a good diet, get plenty of sleep, and cultivate healthy relationships. Studies have shown that engaging in mindful activities at work, such as going for a brief stroll, making a list of five things you see around you, or naming two fragrances, can actually enhance productivity.

- Give it to yourself. Do you want your positive habits to become permanent? According to numerous studies, rewarding yourself is essential. When we are deprived of something, we begin to rationalise and excuse our undesirable behaviour. This frequently sounds like "I've earned this" or "I deserve this," and it's frequently the beginning of the end of our growth; yet, it is typically the beginning of the end of our progress. Instead, reward your hard work with small rewards at various intervals during your self-discipline practise. These luxuries, whether in the form of a delicious meal or a fresh pair of shoes, will ensure that you never feel drained, depleted, or deprived in any way.

- Give yourself forgiveness. It is equally essential that you can forgive yourself when you make a mistake. In number eight of the last section, we discussed the fact that your failure is unavoidable. The fact that you have moved on is the most important thing. To accomplish this, you need to forgive yourself. A buddy of mine recently shared with me the following advice: "It's not about giving oneself the grace to fall short of expectations." Realistically perceiving everything is the goal. If you oversleep, hurry to work, and forget to bring your coffee, which forces you to spend 30 minutes chatting with coworkers in the break room and leaves you three prospect calls shy of your day's goal, you need to take a realistic view of the issue. Have you been unable to achieve what you set out to do? If yes, will you need to place a couple more calls first thing in the morning? Probably. Will this have any kind of bearing on how far you get in the long run? Nope. After analysing the consequences of your detour, you will be able to decide how to proceed and get back on the right path. Step one? Before you turn in for the night, check that your alarm is set. Keep in mind that developing self-discipline takes time and effort. You can't expect yourself to be flawless every single day. The most important thing is to show up each day ready to give it a shot. Therefore, what adjustments do you plan to make to your routine today?

Conclusion

Do you have the desire to achieve greatness? As a result, you have to come to terms with the fact that you are the source of your amazing potential. If you want to be successful in life, you need to shift your mindset and develop habits that will serve you well along the way. Only then can you hope to achieve your goals. Keeping one's distance from the pack is an example of one such practice.

Never let fear prevent you from being the genuine, authentic version of yourself, regardless of what you believe other people want you to be. Being one of a kind indeed comes with its fair share of difficulties, but the rewards far outweigh those difficulties by a wide margin.

Investigate the approaches taken by individuals who have attained a degree of success that is comparable to your own. Experts in their fields who possess specialized knowledge are in constant demand and are held in high esteem by everyone from commoners to rulers of the state.

Not to mention the fact that the inspiration to advance and push to improve oneself as part of the process of maturing into a person is a continual one. It requires making constant investments in oneself by maintaining a high degree of self-awareness, determining areas of one's life that may be improved, and taking efforts to achieve those improvements to be successful. Both technical and soft skills are welcome in this section of the application

ABOUT THE AUTHOR

He is an activist. He was born in Lilongwe, Malawi's capital city. He is a former member of the British Armed Forces, a youth advocate, a world civility ambassador, a writer, an entrepreneur, and a community worker. Founder, TDTA, The Drive to Advance Youth Initiative-Malawi, He earned a BA honours politics from Manchester Metropolitan University after studying political science.

He holds a Master's in International Relations and Global Communication. He has intermediate certificates in financial accounting from Emile Wolf, as well as certificates in information technology (ICT). He also holds certificates in logistics and supply from the Defence Logistics Supply School, Deep Cut. He has taken courses in diplomacy and several strategic leadership and governance courses

He is a former British Army soldier, the director of Malawi Heritage UK, the former chairman of the Labour Party in Openshaw and Clayton, the former vice chairman and one of the founders of the Malawi Congress Party Global Diaspora Network, the former and first chairperson of the Malawi Congress Party UK chapter, the editor of the Malawi Daily Telegraph, an executive member of the London Political Summit, a member of the Manchester School Governors Association, the school governor of Ravensbury Primary, and a guest board member of the Stockport Homes Governance Board.

In 2023, he achieved a great accomplishment by earning his honorary doctorate of philosophy in the humanities from the United Graduate College and Seminary International, USA. This recognition is a testament to his dedication and hard work towards promoting youth and civility in many countries. In 2019, at the 21st Gathering of Africa's Best (GAB) Awards, held at the Manchester Hilton, he received an award of excellence from Trumpet Media Groups. He also received a Greatness University 2020 World Book of Greatness for his community service and contribution to making a difference. CHARISMA honoured him with the Manchester Peace Award.

He is happily married to his wife, Sonja, a Jamaican.

Printed in Great Britain
by Amazon

23547288R00110